Quest
(The Search for Heroes)

Hero Quest • Servant Quest • Character Quest

PRETEEN ELECTIVES
AGES 10-12

A Curriculum for Preteens

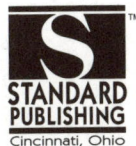

STANDARD PUBLISHING
Cincinnati, Ohio

Quest
(The Search for Heroes)

About the Authors

Mike Thompson is a children's minister who has spent the past eleven years working with young people of all ages. During this time, he has focused especially on the needs of elementary and upper elementary kids through teaching, writing lessons, and related activities.

Cindy Thompson is a homemaker and writer. For thirteen years she taught upper elementary children in public schools. She has also served as a teen youth sponsor and a Sunday school teacher for elementary-age kids.

Lea Clark is a sixth grade school teacher at Christ Centered School. A 1992 graduate of Milligan College, she holds a BS in elementary education. Lea is married and currently lives in Cincinnati, Ohio.

Sandra Wagner Horine is a Christian Education Director. Her experience with preteens comes from many years of teaching Sunday school and Vacation Bible School, leading children's youth groups, and counseling at children's summer camps. Her writing experience includes co-authoring a children's communion curriculum. She is married and has two preschool daughters, Annalisa and Allyson.

Cover design and illustration by Brian Lemke
Inside illustrations by Brian Lemke/Sherry F. Willbrand

The Standard Publishing Company, Cincinnati, Ohio
A Division of Standex International Corporation
©1996 The Standard Publishing Company
All rights reserved
Printed in the United States of America

03 02 01 00 99 98 97 96   5 4 3 2 1
ISBN 0-7847-0503-8

Quest (The Search for Heroes)

Beyond childhood, heading to the next level, preteens choose others to follow. Help them choose appropriate heroes. Help them become Christlike examples. Help them learn the secrets to winning in real life!

Unit 1   Hero Quest   8

Written by Mike and Cynthia Thompson to help kids build respect for appropriate real-life heroes.

Unit 2   Servant Quest   42

Written by Lea Clark to encourage kids to develop service skills and become servant heroes.

Unit 3   Character Quest   76

Written by Sandra F. Horine to lead kids to identify character qualities of biblical heroes.

Why "Next Level"?

Upper elementary kids—we'll call them preteens—are reaching, striving, groping toward the next level. They're in transition. They want to be taller, stronger, faster, and smarter as they catapult on their way to the next level.

In some ways preteens appear already to have arrived at the next level (once termed junior high). Preteens want to wear the right clothes, match hairstyles with athletes or rock stars, and fit in with the peer group no matter what! For many, however, the next level is an elusive goal: manly muscles and feminine curves are controlled by hormones not purchasing power.

So, too, the limits on thought structure. Many, if not most, fifth and sixth graders lack the ability to think critically, form logical arguments, or draw general principles from specific examples. There is usually a wide gulf between their level of experience and their ability to reflect on the meaning of their experiences.

Preteens are also still resolving the issue: *What can I do well?* rather than tackling the adolescent question: *Who am I?* So when preteens dress and act like their peers, they are striving for self-acceptance—feeling that they are as up-to-date as their peers, rather than endeavoring to establish a personal identity. Erickson's studies show that ten to twelve year olds are less involved with establishing a personal identity than they are with figuring out what they're really good at. This disparity creates difficulties for those using junior high curriculum for preteen classes: "What you see (a teenager) is not what you get (concrete-operational thinking and a different life task)."

Next Level curriculum is transitional: to help transitional preteens feel comfortable in teen-style learning settings and to equip leaders to teach within the limits of a preteen's limited development. Sessions are structured to help you teach preteens effectively in groups. The younger the student, the more discussion guidance must be given to identify appropriate conclusions and to suggest appropriate actions to be taken.

While many junior high topics are helpful and many elective curriculums look age appropriate, they often do not work with preteens because they were not designed for their limited thought processing and inexperienced discussion skills.

Next Level Preteen Electives! Planned and designed with preteen issues in mind and tailored for the learning capabilities of concrete thinkers! Visually appealing for the video generation. Emotionally satisfying for techno-driven kids.

This curriculum offers bonus opportunities for preteens to **Go to Extremes** serving others. It also strives to build family relationships—**Bridge the Gap**—during fun-filled family sessions.

So, because life is not a game—
pick a topic and recruit some helpers.
Start a group for ten to twelve year olds—
They'll be glad you did!

Next Level Preteen Electives address the importance of instilling values for character development.

This curriculum includes positive, choice-making strategies, friendship-making skills, care-giving and service skills, as well as refusal strategies (when appropriate). Each preteen in the program should feel accepted, important, and supported!

Surveys of Christian educators, Sunday school teachers, and Christian parents encourage us not to abandon the teaching of fundamentals. That's why Next Level curriculum includes units designed to equip kids to use the Bible, offers a survey of Bible heroes, and help kids fit in at church, among other topics. Future books will build mission awareness, encourage a strong sense of biblical stewardship, and help kids reconnect with adults who will guide them to maturity.

You can use Next Level Preteen Electives confidently, knowing that it is based on core biblical principles, permeated with Bible teaching, and presented in a way that ten to twelve year olds can understand and enjoy!

How are Next Level units organized?

Get Into the Game

As an introduction to the session, this section offers activities to grab the students' attention and encourage participation from the entire group.

These lesson steps offer activity choices that may be set up as learning centers or used as options. Depending on the class size, the teacher may divide the class into smaller groups to complete the activity. Each group works on the activity. For this to be effective, ample assistance is needed.

If the class is small, the teacher can customize the session to fit that need. Select one or two options to utilize or have the class work together instead of dividing into small groups.

Step 1

The activity is designed to help students dig deeper into the topic.

Step 2

This section offers another way to discover biblical truth.

Step 3

This activity involves the entire class to help students apply what was learned in Steps 1 and 2.

Take It to the Next Level

This final section concludes the session by helping students commit the principles they have learned to their own lives. The question, "So what does this mean to me personally?" can be answered in this section.

Extra Helps

Each unit introduction includes devotion suggestions for either the teacher and/or the students. The devotional ideas correlate with the sessions contained in that particular unit.

Reproducible pages are provided for your convenience. Photocopy these pages for your personal use or for your students' use to enhance each session.

Additional Resources

The following list of books, videos, and music serve as extra resources for each unit. Feel free to use these materials as research prior to teaching or as extra activities if you deem appropriate.

Books

The Book of Virtues by William J. Bennett, Simon & Schuster
How to Be a Hero to Your Kids by Josh McDowell and Dick Day, Word Publishing
Real Heroes devotionals by Tim Hansel, Chariot
Florence Nightingale by Sandy Dengler, Moody
The Trailblazers series by Dave and Neta Jackson, Bethany House
Today's Heroes Series (ages 8-12), Zondervan. (The series includes Dennis Byrd, Chuck Colson, Andre Dawson, Dave Johnson, Colin Powell, Joni Eareckson Tada, and Heather Whitestone.)
Bible Hero Read and Do Activities, Standard Publishing (Heroes include Joseph, Moses, Daniel, Esther, Mary and Elizabeth, Peter, and Paul.)
Bible Hero Reproducible Activity Books, Standard Publishing (Heroes include John the Baptist, Mary, Paul, and Peter.)

Videos

Bible Hero Videos (Hanna Barbera)
Dravecky (A Story of Courage and Grace) by Dave Dravecky, Zondervan

Music

"Heart of a Hero" by Petra (Word)
"Hero" by Steve Taylor (Warner Alliance)
"The Lion's Den" by Guardian (Myrrh)
"I Am a Servant" by Larry Norman (Sonrise Music/Benson)
"Serve Somebody" by Johnny Q. Public (Gotee)
"Seize the Day" by Carolyn Arends (Reunion)

Hero Quest

Helping Preteens Choose Heroes

In a recent survey of 145,000 students conducted by *Weekly Reader,* only 48 percent knew that Albert Gore was the vice president of the United States, while 84 percent of the same students knew that Bart Simpson's sister's name was Lisa. This information may cause one to ask questions like, "Where did we go wrong? How did this generation of children get blown so far off course morally?" An even better question would be, "What are we going to do about it?" When fictitious characters who have no moral character are recognized by our children more than their leaders, it is time to examine our children's choices of heroes and the thought processes involved in those choices.

It has been said that today's children do not have heroes like the children of previous generations. Many ask, "Where have all of our heroes gone?" The answer to this question is, "They have been replaced by celebrities." Children are choosing heroes all of the time, and what should concern us is the criteria kids use to select their heroes. In other words, why are the Simpsons more popular than the vice president? According to Christian author Dave Jackson, "Celebrities are big images

Session 1—
Hero Worship: How to Choose Your Heroes

Know the difference between acceptable and unacceptable heroes.

Feel capable of recognizing whether hero choices are based on the world's standards or God's standards.

Select heroes to imitate and admire based upon what God says in His Word.

Session 2—
A Hero or a Zero? Qualities of Heroes

Know the positive qualities to seek in selecting responsible, godly heroes.

Feel convinced that the qualities of true heroes are found in God's Word.

Evaluate the characteristics of today's heroes.

Session 3—
Who, Me, a Hero?

Know that being a hero involves action.

Feel a sense of responsibility concerning their personal actions and example.

Become heroes by obeying God's Word, serving others, and influencing others by their example.

Session 4—
The Ultimate Hero—Jesus

Know that Jesus is their Hero through His example in life, His sacrificial death, and His supernatural resurrection.

Feel Jesus' unique love and value for them.

Strive to imitate Christ daily by valuing others and being unselfish.

created by the media" (see *Christian Parenting Today,* "Heroes and Impostors," November/December 1994, pp. 26-33). Often these celebrities are lacking or devoid of moral character and a positive life-style. The difference between heroes and celebrities, according to Jackson, is that "heroes are distinguished by achievement, particularly deeds of moral achievement."

In this unit on helping preteens choose heroes, it is vital that you communicate that difference to your students. Realizing this difference will aid them in seeking to honor God in their choices of heroes. Instead of being influenced by their peers and the standards of popular culture, your students need to be guided instead by God's Word when it comes to choosing heroes. Another factor resulting from this unit will be an attempt on the part of your students to become heroes themselves by being obedient to God's Word, by being positive examples to others, and by serving others. Finally, your students will come to see Jesus as their supreme Hero, and will seek to honor Him as they live.

As you prepare to teach this unit, be mindful that one of the main goals is for your preteens to walk away knowing what God says about each session topic. Games and activities are provided to reinforce the biblical perspective. The reproducible sheets will be your helpful tools in initiating discussion.

As you review the sessions, be sure to gather materials needed well in advance. This will ensure maximum use of your time with the students. You'll want to have Bibles, pencils, and paper on hand for each session. Substitute a large sheet of paper and markers for a chalkboard.

When preparing the sessions, keep the developmental abilities of preteens in mind. This age group loves competition, so be sure to take advantage of the games provided. Because kids in this group are beginning to experience physical and emotional changes, they are prone to mood swings. Don't let this deter you in your efforts. Preteens may react differently to different things. As you prepare, remember that preteens are eager to learn. Challenge them to think by asking questions and encouraging discussion about what God has to say about their choices of heroes. Keep in mind also that peer pressure is ever-present in the lives of preteens. Friendship with peers becomes the most important relationship for them, so it is crucial for kids in this age to choose the same heroes that their friends are choosing (according to Dave Jackson). These choices result in their attempt to "display characteristics which will create a favorable impression" among their peers. Thus, it becomes important to wear the right clothes, have the right sports cards, etc. Preteens have three choices: to try to do without heroes, to imitate bad role models, or to follow heroes who exhibit moral character and a positive lifestyle.

It is your mission (and your privilege) to help them desire to imitate positive heroes because of what God's Word tells them. Where have all the heroes gone? They're still out there, and preteens will imitate them if we can help point them in the right direction. It's a worthwhile mission, one that can be enjoyable as well.

Daily Devotions

To round out this unit, the following schedule of daily devotions is provided for you and your preteen students. Encourage them to read the Scriptures and reflect upon their choices of heroes, the qualities of those heroes, how they can be heroes to others, and upon their Ultimate Hero—Jesus. Encourage them also to pray about their choices of heroes and to ask for wisdom in making choices that would please Him.

Week 1	Week 2	Week 3	Week 4
Hero Worship How to Choose Your Heroes	**A Hero or a Zero?** Qualities of Heroes	**Who, Me, a Hero?**	**The Ultimate Hero —Jesus**
Monday Proverbs 3:31, 32	**Monday** 2 Peter 1:5, 6	**Monday** 1 Timothy 4:12	**Monday** Mark 10:45
Tuesday Acts 6:1-7	**Tuesday** 2 Peter 1:7, 8	**Tuesday** Hebrews 6:10-12	**Tuesday** 1 Peter 3:18
Wednesday James 4:4	**Wednesday** Romans 12:10-13	**Wednesday** 1 Peter 2:9	**Wednesday** Ephesians 5:1, 2
Thursday 2 Thessalonians 3:6, 7	**Thursday** Romans 12:14-16	**Thursday** Colossians 3: 12- 17	**Thursday** John 13: 15
Friday Hebrews 13:7	**Friday** Galatians 5:22, 23	**Friday** Joshua 24:15	**Friday** Philippians 2:5-11
Saturday 3 John 11	**Saturday** 3 John 11	**Saturday** 3 John 11	**Saturday** 3 John 11

Session 1

Hero Worship: How to Choose Your Heroes

Get Into the Game

Before the session, write the various actions for the students to imitate on slips of paper and place each one in a sealed envelope.

Suggested actions to imitate

bark like a dog

drop to the floor and do ten push-ups

walk over to your youth leader and say, "Holy copycats, Batman"

suck your thumb like a baby

sing "This Little Light of Mine" and do the motions

untie your shoe, then retie it

turn all the chairs in the room upside down

pretend you are snow skiing

After the students arrive, tell them to choose a partner. Give each pair a sealed envelope and inform them that it is to be opened by one partner, who must follow the instructions written on the paper. The second partner must imitate the actions of the first partner. Each pair must act out their written instructions. After the last pair finishes (and the chairs are all picked up again), have the students take their seats. Ask them the following questions:

1. How did you feel when you were carrying out your instructions?

2. What was it like having someone imitate your every move?

Ask the second partners the following questions:

1. How did you feel having to imitate your partner without seeing the instructions?

2. Would you rather have had a choice of whom to imitate?

Allow time for responses and discussion.

Scripture. Proverbs 3:31, 32; Acts 6:1-7; 2 Thessalonians 3:6, 7; Hebrews 13:7; James 4:4

Know the difference between acceptable and unacceptable heroes.

Feel capable of recognizing whether hero choices are based on the world's standards or God's standards.

Select heroes to imitate and admire based upon what God says in His Word.

Materials

nine envelopes with written instructions inside

Step 1

Before the session, collect sports cards of famous athletes, and pictures of famous celebrities (you can cut these pictures out of magazines such as *Time, People,* or *Seventeen*). Spread the cards and pictures out on a table and instruct the students to select one card or picture.

After they make their selection, write these two questions on the board:
1. Why did you select the picture you have?
2. Would you consider this person to be a hero today? Why?

Give the kids a minute to think about their answers, and then call on them to respond. Encourage and affirm them as much as possible as they share with the group. After they respond, say: "Today we are going to learn about the heroes we choose to honor and imitate. As we think about heroes, we will also try to understand what influences us as we make those choices. Because we are seeking to be like Jesus, we also want to see if our choices of heroes are acceptable to God. The best way to do this is to read the Bible to see what God says about the people we choose to consider as heroes."

Materials
sports cards of famous athletes, pictures of celebrities, chalkboard, chalk

Step 2

In a group setting, read and discuss the Scriptures and questions provided on the reproducible sheet, "Scripture Quest" on page 15. When reading the Scriptures, be sure to have Bibles handy. A modern translation such as the *New International Version* would be the most effective.

These Scriptures deal with the choices that are involved in being a friend of God, and how those choices relate to pre-teens' selections of heroes today.

Some possible answers follow.

Materials
photocopies of page 15

Acts 6:1-7

1. What problem occurred in verses 1, 2? (Widows weren't being cared for.)

2. What choices were made in order to solve the problem (verses 3-5)? (Choose men full of wisdom and the Spirit and delegate the responsibility to them so the others could teach and pray.)

3. Why do you think these seven men were chosen to help? Do you think that people in that time considered them to be heroes? Do heroes always have to be famous or can they be people who seem ordinary? (These men were chosen on the basis of their character and conviction for God. Heroes can be ordinary people—not just celebrities.)

4. What happened as a result of the choices made? (The word of God spread; the church grew.)

Hebrews 13:7

1. Name a leader that you would consider to be a hero today. What makes that person a hero in your mind?

2. According to this verse, there are three reasons why we should remember our leaders. List them. Are these reasons important to you as you select heroes today? (They spoke the word of God to us; they had faith; their lives were good examples with good results.)

After the students have answered the questions, summarize what they have learned about hero choices based on biblical standards.

Step 3

This activity encourages students to evaluate their hero choices based on God's Word. Distribute copies of the reproducible sheet "Dear Hero" on page 16, along with Bibles and pencils.

Materials
photocopies of page 16

Have students read Proverbs 3:31, 32; 2 Thessalonians 3:6, 7; and James 4:4. After students have read these Scriptures aloud, ask the following questions:

1. How does God feel about violent people? (Proverbs 3:32)

2. What two things are we warned to "keep away" from in 2 Thessalonians 3:6, 7? (Those who are idle and do not follow God's teachings.)

3. In James 4:4, why is "friendship with the world" considered to be "hatred toward God"? (When we follow the world, we turn our backs on God.)

4. What are some things that today's heroes do that might displease God?" (Commit adultery; take God's name in vain; hurt people to gain position.)

After the students have had time to answer the questions, ask them to fill out the reproducible sheet. Tell them to write a letter to someone they consider to be a hero. They should tell these heroes *why* they admire them so much. Then in the second letter, they are to explain why they might admire them more if they changed some of their behavior. They can write the letters to one person or two separate people. For example:

"Dear Jim Harbaugh, I admire you because you're a great quarterback and you led the Indianapolis Colts to the AFC Championship game. I especially admire you because you always thank your Lord and Savior, Jesus Christ, in every post-game interview. That makes you a hero to me!"

"Dear Courteney Cox, I admire you because you're very pretty and you're funny on the TV show, 'Friends.' But I would

admire you even more if you'd stop using God's name in vain in your show. It's not necessary, and it sets a bad example. You can still be funny without doing that!"

Encourage students to be honest and choose people they really like. They should write the letters with the Scripture references in mind. Allow the students to read their letters to the rest of the class. Then say, "It's OK to admire people for the talents God has given them, even if they don't realize that their talents are from God. But we must always keep the singing, acting, or athletic ability in perspective. That ability is only a part of that person. We have to decide if they're using their talents and living their lives for God and His glory."

Take It to the Next Level

Say, "Think about the choices of celebrities and athletes you made earlier. Would you consider these heroes to be acceptable to God? Why or why not? Why do you think that God is concerned about the heroes you choose?"

After the students discuss these questions, have each of them read 3 John 11. Ask, "What does this verse say concerning our choices of heroes?"

After they answer, ask, "Do you see now why your choices of heroes matter to the Lord? He loves you, and He wants you to enjoy the life He's given you. One way we can enjoy life is by making wise choices of heroes to follow and imitate."

Give students the following assignment. Tell them to look through magazines this coming week to find stories or pictures of godly heroes. Encourage the students to bring their findings to the next session.

Close with prayer, thanking God for giving us choices of whom to follow and imitate, and also asking for wisdom in making future choices of heroes.

Scripture Quest

**Read the following Scriptures and answer
the corresponding questions.**

Read Acts 6:1-7

1. What problem occurred in verses 1, 2?

2. What choices were made in order to solve the problem (verses 3-5)?

3. Why do you think these seven men were chosen to help?
Do you think that people in that time considered them to be heroes?
Do heroes always have to be famous or can they be people who seem ordinary?

4. What happened as a result of the choices made?

Read Hebrews 13:7

1. Name a leader that you would consider to be a hero today.
What makes him or her a hero in your mind?

2. According to this verse, what are the reasons
we should remember our leaders?
List them. Are these reasons important
to you as you select heroes today?

Dear Hero...

Dear _____,

I admire you because . . .

Signed,

Q

Dear _____,

I would admire you more if . . .

Signed,

Q

A Hero or a Zero? Qualities of Heroes

Scripture. Romans 12:10-16; Galatians 5:22, 23; 2 Peter 1:5-8

Know the positive qualities to seek in selecting responsible, godly heroes.
Feel convinced that the qualities of true heroes are found in God's Word.
Evaluate the characteristics of today's heroes.

Get Into the Game

Before the session, gather materials for a unique scavenger hunt. During this activity, the students will be searching for particular "qualities." The scavenger hunt can be held inside and/or outside the church building, but you will need to do some preparatory work to ensure its success. To avoid confusion, make sure you gather all of your materials beforehand. The goal of the scavenger hunt is to collect as many positive qualities as possible within a fifteen-minute time limit. The qualities can be found in the Scriptures that you and the students will study together later (Romans 12:10-16; Galatians 5:22, 23; 2 Peter 1:5-8).

Divide your group into two teams and give each team a copy of the items they must find. Give them fifteen minutes and have them report back to you with their findings. Feel free to use your own creativity, or you can use the items on the "Quality Scavenger Hunt" list (page 20).

After fifteen minutes, call time and allow teams to gather together. The team with the most items collected gets to open their bag of M&M's candy and share with their teammates. The team with the least amount of items collected must wait until after the meeting to open their candy. In the event of a tie, both teams can open their candy immediately.

While they are eating their candy, discuss the scavenger hunt. Ask, "How did you feel when you were searching for these items? Was it worth it?" Allow time for the students to respond. Say, "Last week we learned that there are many different reasons why people are considered heroes. Not all reasons please God. Today we are going to learn about the kinds of qualities we are to look for in heroes—the qualities that

Materials

two copies of instructions for "Quality Scavenger Hunt," two of the following items: church bulletin or church directory, dictionary or encyclopedia, M&M's candy, leaf or acorn, Bible, hymnal or songbook, rose, a watch or clock, a blanket or pillow, baby toy or stuffed animal would please God. Choosing heroes with the right qualities is a lot like finding the items needed for your scavenger hunt. It's not easy, but it's certainly worthwhile. Let's see what God has to say about the qualities we are to look for in our heroes."

Step 1

Have each student choose a partner to work with on the "Quality Quest Quiz" page. Review the questions with the entire group, but allow them to share their responses with their partner. Following each question, select one pair to share their responses with the entire group.

After you have discussed the Scriptures and questions, focus on the students' choices of heroes. Say, "When we choose our heroes, it's important to know what God's Word says about the kinds of qualities they are to possess." Ask, "Why do you think we should choose godly people as our heroes?" Allow time for the students to respond.

Materials
photocopies of page 21

Step 2

Distribute copies of "Quality Quest Code." Encourage students to work individually on this sheet instead of in pairs.

After allowing plenty of time for the students to finish, have someone look up Galatians 5:22, 23 and read it aloud. Say, "Do you know why these qualities are described as fruit?" Allow time for responses. "Just as a tree can be identified by the fruit on its branches, we can be identified by the example we show to others. If we are growing the way God would desire us to grow, then we would have these characteristics."

Have another student read 2 Peter 1:5-8. Ask, "What is the result of people who possess these qualities?" (They will be effective and productive in God's kingdom.)

Afterwards say, "A true hero is one whose life displays moral character, obedience to God, and a positive lifestyle." In our next activity, we will decide whether someone is heroic or not based upon these qualities."

Materials
photocopies of page 22

Step 3

Divide the group into two teams. Give each team an equal number of "H's" and "0's" (you will need to cut these out of construction paper before class and have them ready). After reading a description of a particular person, one team will decide whether or not that person's actions are those of a hero or those of a zero. Depending upon their decision, the team will place either an "H" or a "0" on the tic-tac-toe grid (for a

Materials
tic-tac-toe grid, ten construction paper H's and 0's (five per team), written descriptions for game, masking tape

grid you can simply put pieces of masking tape on the floor). The game is played until the entire grid is filled. There are no winning or losing teams. Use the descriptions written below.

1. Judas Iscariot betrayed Jesus for thirty pieces of silver. **Hero or zero?**

2. Billy has just moved to town. Today is his first day in the youth group. Everyone ignores him except for Jamie, Phil, and Maurice. **Heroes or zeroes?**

3. Faced with the choice to worship a man-made god or be punished, Daniel chose to remain faithful to the one, true God. **Hero or zero?**

4. Emily looks on Matt's paper and copies his answers during the vocabulary test without getting caught. **Hero or zero?**

5. Barnabas owned a field. When he heard that there were people without food and shelter, he sold his field and gave the money to help those in need. **Hero or zero?**

6. God told Eve to listen to Him and she would be happy. Eve listened to Satan instead and did what she wanted to do. **Hero or zero?**

7. Terence's leg is in a cast. He has a hard time moving fast. At the amusement park, the rest of his group doesn't want to wait for him. Alex, however, stays back and waits with Terence throughout the day. **Hero or zero?**

8. Jenny is at school getting ready to eat lunch. All of the other kids in her class eat without praying. At the risk of being teased, Jenny prays before eating anyway. **Hero or zero?**

9. Stephen was being stoned to death for talking about Jesus, but Stephen prayed for those who were killing him. **Hero or zero?**

After the activity is completed, say, "How did you decide whether or not the person was a hero or a zero?" Allow time for response. Say, "Remember that the Bible tells about both heroes and zeroes. We can learn from both examples."

Take It to the Next Level

Ask the students to present any photos or stories they may have found that represent godly heroes. Tell them that they will have a new assignment to do this week. Tell the students that before the next session, each one must interview at least three people and ask, "What are some qualities you feel a hero should possess?" The people being interviewed cannot be related to the students. Encourage the students to record the responses and be ready to report their answers in next week's session.

Close with prayer, thanking God and asking Him for wisdom as we choose heroes with solid qualities.

Quality Scavenger Hunt

1. Find a church bulletin or directory to represent *faithfulness.*

2. Find an object that represents *knowledge* (i.e. a dictionary or encyclopedia).

3. Find the bag of M&M's candy that I've hidden, and show your *self-control* by not eating any.

4. Find an object of nature that shows *perseverance* (i.e. a leaf from a tree or an acorn, which represents how they grow back every spring).

5. Find a Bible to represent *godliness.*

6. Find a songbook or hymnal to represent *joy.*

7. Find a rose to represent *love.*

8. Find a watch or clock to represent *patience.*

9. Find a blanket or pillow to represent *peace.*

10. Find a baby toy or stuffed animal to represent *gentleness.*

Quality Quest Quiz

1. Of the qualities listed in Romans 12:10-16 *(NIV)*, check the ones most important to you. (Be ready to explain why.)

_____ A. Be devoted to each other (v. 10)
_____ B. Honor each other above yourselves (v. 10)
_____ C. Keep your spiritual enthusiasm (v. 11)
_____ D. Be joyful in hope (v. 12)
_____ E. Patient in affliction (v. 12)
_____ F. Faithful in prayer (v. 12)
_____ G. Share with needy people (v. 13)
_____ H. Practice hospitality (v. 13)
_____ I. Bless those who persecute you (v. 14)
_____ J. Rejoice with those who rejoice (v. 15)
_____ K. Mourn with those who mourn (v. 15)
_____ L. Live in harmony with each other (v. 16)
_____ M. Spend time with people of low position (v. 16)
_____ N. Don't be conceited (v. 16)

2. Do your current heroes possess any of the qualities listed above? Which ones?

3. Do you think these qualities are realistic ones for heroes to have? Why or why not?

Quality Quest Code

A	C	D	E	F	G
1	2	3	4	5	6

H	I	J	K	L	N	O
7	8	9	10	11	12	13

P	R	S	T	U	V	Y
14	15	16	17	18	19	20

1. __ __ __ __ - __ __ __ __ __ __ __
    16 4 11 5   2 13 12 17 15 13 11

2. __ __ __ __
    11 13 19 4

3. __ __ __ __ __ __ __ __ __ __
    6 4 12 17 11 4 12 4 16 16

4. __ __ __
    9 13 20

5. __ __ __ __ __ __ __ __ __ __ __ __
    5 1 8 17 7 5 18 11 12 4 16 16

6. __ __ __ __ __
    14 4 1 2 4

7. __ __ __ __ __ __ __ __
    6 13 13 3 12 4 16 16

8. __ __ __ __ __ __ __ __
    14 1 17 8 4 12 2 4

9. __ __ __ __ __ __ __ __
    10 8 12 3 12 4 16 16

Use the code to find the qualities or "fruit of the Spirit" listed in Galatians 5:22, 23 *(NIV).*

Session 3

Who, Me, a Hero?

Scripture. 1 Timothy 4:12; Colossians 3:12-17; Joshua 24:15

Know that being a hero involves action.
Feel a sense of responsibility concerning their personal actions and example.
Become heroes by obeying God's Word, serving others, and influencing others by their example.

Get Into the Game

Before the session, set up a volleyball net (indoors or outdoors depending upon your facility). Cover the net with sheets or blankets so that the students cannot see the other side. As the students arrive, tell them that they are going to play "Blind Volleyball." It's exactly like regular volleyball, with the exception that you can't see what's on the other side of the net. Divide teams and play until interest fades, then call time and meet together again. After everyone is back together, ask, "How did it feel to play volleyball without being able to see the other team?" Allow time for students to respond. Then ask, "What was it like when it came your turn to serve and you couldn't see where the ball was going? What if you had decided not to serve because you couldn't see where the ball might go?" Again, allow time for players to respond.

After student responses, say, "Sometimes we may feel that our lives are like the game we just played. Sometimes we may feel that serving God and serving others is worthless because we can't see the outcome of our service." Ask, "Have you ever felt this way before? Have you ever felt like you were a hero when you served God or other people in the past?" Say, "You may not realize it, but when you choose to obey God, to serve others, and to be an example to others, you are a hero in His sight. Even though you might not be able to see the end result, God honors you."

Say, "In the last two sessions, we discovered how to choose our heroes and what qualities to look for in heroes. In today's session, we'll learn how we can be heroes to others. It starts with a choice we make to serve God and others by the way we live."

Materials

volleyball, volleyball net, blankets or sheets

Step 1

Provide each student with a pencil and the reproducible sheet "Never Too Young to Serve." Allow time for students to read the Scripture and complete the page. You may need to help students with a word such as *purity*.

Some possible answers are:

1. Speech—saying "please" and "thank you," not using God's name as a swear word, not lying

2. Life—letting others go first, obeying your parents and teachers, doing your homework

3. Love—getting along with your brothers and sisters, doing an errand for a neighbor, going to visit a sick friend

4. Faith—going to church every Sunday, reading your Bible daily, memorizing Scripture

5. Purity—not watching R-rated videos, saying *only* good things about people, not telling off-color jokes and stories

When all the students have finished, ask volunteers to share some of their answers. Encourage your students to put the things they have listed into practice.

Materials
photocopies of page 26

Step 2

Distribute copies of the reproducible sheet "What Does a Hero Look Like?" Then divide the students into three groups. Tell each group to read Colossians 3:12-17 then describe a hero using the characteristics from the Scripture. Each group can have a different answer, as long as each answer uses all or most of the following characteristics: compassion, kindness, humility, gentleness, patience, forgiveness, love, peace, and thankfulness.

Here are some possible descriptions:

1. Ears that will listen as long as they need to do so (patience).

2. Arms that will lift a small, crying child (kindness, gentleness, or compassion).

3. Feet that will go next door to check on an elderly neighbor (kindness, love, or compassion).

4. A mouth that says, "I'm sorry" (forgiveness, humility).

Give the students as many examples as they need, but encourage them to be original and come up with their own ideas.

After everyone is finished, have one student from each group read the description. Ask students, "Whether we are serving others or being an example to others, what should our attitude be?" (Colossians 3:17).

Say, "You've seen what God's Word says about how you can

Materials
photocopies of page 27

be a hero, but you can't be a hero unless you choose to do so. In our next activity, you'll get the chance to encourage one another to choose to be a hero for the Lord."

Step 3

Divide the students into three groups. Instruct them that each group will be given an assignment to do based on being a hero.

Group #1 will create a commercial on how to be a hero by listening to God (obeying His Word).

Group #2 will create and act out a skit on how to be a hero by serving others.

Group #3 will create and perform a song about how to be a hero by being an example for others.

Provide paper and pencils in case students need to outline their presentations or jot down notes. Give each group fifteen minutes to prepare and then have them share their creations. Have a video camera ready to film each group's performance. Afterwards, play the tape back for the entire group to watch.

Following this, ask, "How did it feel when you were performing? What was it like seeing yourself on the tape?" Say, "What you did a few minutes ago was a performance, but when you listen to God, when you serve others, and when you are an example for others, you aren't performing. You are being a hero for God. You don't have to do great things that are noticed by everyone in order to be a hero. You are a hero when you do the little things that are important. Things like serving people, being an example, and being obedient to God."

Materials
paper, video camera, blank video cassette, TV

Take It to the Next Level

Read Joshua 24:15 together. Say, "Being a hero begins by making choices to obey God, to serve others, and to influence others."

Give each student a chocolate gold coin. Say, "This is your gold medal. You, too, can be a hero if you choose to do so."

Ask the students to present the results from their interviews. Then give them the next assignment. Say, "This week I want you to look for ways to be a hero by obeying God, serving others, and influencing others. Be ready to report on at least one way you were able to do this." You may want to have students suggest ways they could do this (read Bible, pray, go to church, help someone with homework, open doors for others, let others go first in line, run an errand for an elderly person).

Close with prayer, thanking God for giving you the chance to be one of His heroes.

Materials
chocolate gold coins

Never Too Young to Serve!

List ways you can set a good example in the five areas listed in this Scripture.
"Do not let anyone look down on you because you are young, but set an example for the believers in speech, in life, in love, in faith, and in purity."
1 Timothy 4:12

Life _____

Speech _____

Love _____

Purity _____

Faith _____

What Does a Hero Look Like?

Read Colossians 3:12-17. Describe your hero using the characteristics listed in this Scripture. (For example: eyes that see only love, seeing the good in others.) You may have to write a small description for each body part.

The Ultimate Hero—Jesus

Memory Verse

Scripture Mark 10:45; John 13:15; Ephesians 5:1-2; 1 Peter 3:18

Know that Jesus is their Hero through His example in life, His sacrificial death, and His supernatural resurrection.
Feel Jesus' unique love and value for them.
Strive to imitate Christ daily by valuing others and being unselfish.

Get Into the Game

Have the students sit in a circle. Tell them that they will all get the opportunity to be king or queen for a day. When you say "go," they must get up from the circle and go to one of the other students and demand any item that the student has with them. This item can be a purse, comb, shoes, shoelaces, socks, wallet or anything in their pockets. The student must surrender this item to the king or queen who demands it. After a few minutes, gather everyone together in a circle again. One by one have each king or queen show what they took and tell why they wanted it. Then return the items to their rightful owners.

After the items have been returned, tell the students that they will get the opportunity to be slaves for a day. When you say "go," they must leave the circle, find another student and give that student one of their own items. After everyone has given something away, have the students gather together again in a circle. Ask, "How did it feel to take something from someone else simply because you were king or queen? How did it feel to have something taken from you?" Allow time for student responses. Then ask, "How did it feel to willingly sacrifice one of your possessions to another person? What was it like receiving something without expecting it?" Again, allow time for responses.

Say, "Often, those who possess power, money, and popularity are worshiped as heroes. In the game you just played, you saw how leaders sometimes abuse their power for selfish reasons. Jesus is the most powerful person to have walked the earth, yet He did not use that power for himself. Instead, He used it to heal people, to love people, and to save them. That's what being a hero is all about—being unselfish. Today, we'll see why Jesus is the Ultimate Hero and why He is deserving of our honor and love."

Step 1

Say, "Real heroes look out for others first before they look out for themselves. Jesus is the supreme example of unselfishness. Can you name some heroes today who are unselfish?" Allow time for responses. Then say, "Now we're going to discover ways we can imitate Jesus in our daily lives."

Distribute pencils and copies of "Matters of Life and Death." Divide the students into two groups. Have one group read Mark 10:45 and the other group read 1 Peter 3:18. Have each group answer the questions that follow their assigned Scripture. Allow time for the students to answer the questions, then go over them together.

Some possible answers for Mark 10:45:

1. Which is easier, to be served by others or to serve others? Why? (Being served by others is easier because they do all the work.)

2. How does it make you feel to know that Jesus came to serve *you*? (special, honored, humbled, loved)

3. How does Jesus' life compare to the lives of our heroes today? (Most use their positions for their own gain and selfishness; Jesus put others first.)

Some possible answers for 1 Peter 3:18:

· 1. How do you feel about Jesus, knowing that He died for you? Is He a hero to you? (loved, blessed, honored)

2. According to this verse, what happened between you and God as a result of Jesus' death? (I am now one of God's children.)

3. What does Jesus' sacrificial death tell us about His feelings for us? (It was the ultimate act of love.)

Reemphasize, "Real heroes look out for others first before they look out for themselves."

Materials
photocopies of page 31

Step 2

Read Ephesians 5:1, 2, then distribute copies of "Living Sacrifices." Assign students to read the role play situations. Allow time for students to prepare their role plays. Circulate throughout the room and offer assistance when needed.

After the students have performed the role plays, say, "When we imitate God through our lives, we can become heroes like Jesus. He loved us enough to give up His life for us. We should love and care for others the way Jesus did."

Materials
photocopies of page 32

Step 3

String a clothesline across the room in which you are meeting. Instruct the students that you are going to give them two cards, a pen, and a clothespin. On one card, they are to write a short note about the person on their right. The note should read, "You are valuable because . . ." Have the students complete the statement with an encouraging thought about the person on their right. If they do not know that person, they can still write something encouraging about them (i.e., "You are valuable because you have a great smile," or "You are valuable because you can look out for others first as Jesus did"). After they finish their notes of encouragement, they are to write the person's name on the outside of the card and attach it to the clothesline with the clothespin.

On the other card, the students are to write one unselfish thing they can do for someone this week (cleaning their room doesn't count!). After they write this down, have the group share what they will do. Encourage them to follow through with it this week. Say, "Jesus is a hero because of His unselfish example in life and death, but also because He overcame death. Through God's power, Jesus was raised from death. No hero today can top that. Let's make sure we honor Him as our ultimate Hero by continually thanking Him and by valuing others and being unselfish."

Take It to the Next Level

Have students report on the choices they made this week by obeying God, serving others, and influencing others.

Read John 13:15. Encourage students to do one act this week that will imitate Christ. Mention some of the examples given from the session (encouraging others, including others, valuing others).

Close with prayer. Be sure that everyone picks up their encouragement card from the clothesline before they leave.

Materials

clothesline, duct tape, clothespins (one per student), blank cards (two per student), pens (one per student)

Matters of
Life and Death

Read the Scriptures and answer the following questions.

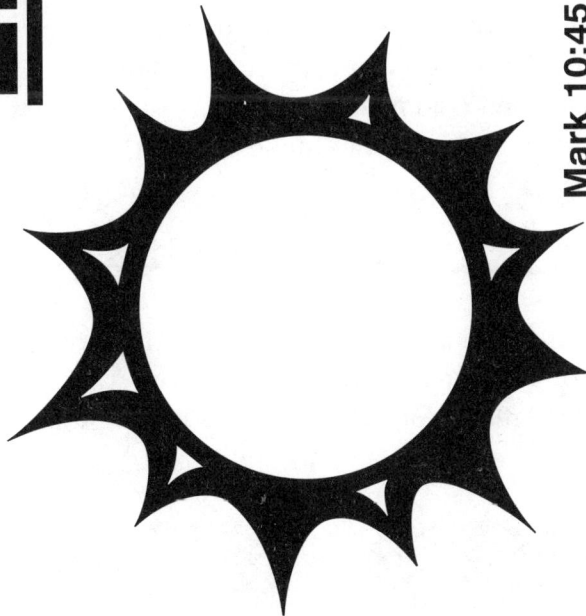

Mark 10:45

1. Which is easier, to be served by others or to serve others? Why?

2. How does it make you feel to know that Jesus came to serve *you*?

3. How does Jesus' life compare to the lives of our heroes today?

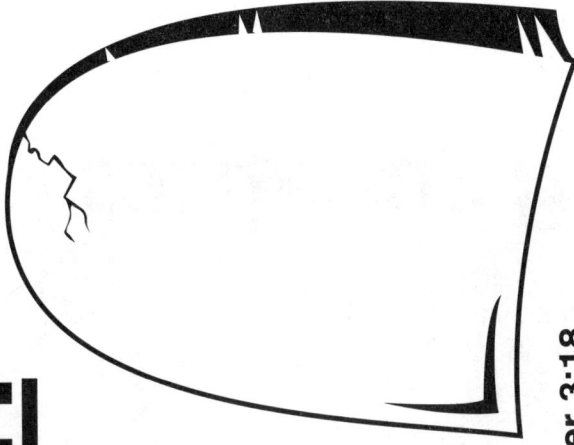

1 Peter 3:18

1. How do you feel about Jesus, knowing that He died for you? Is He a hero to you?

2. According to this verse, what happened between you and God as a result of Jesus' death?

3. What does Jesus' sacrificial death tell us about His feelings for us?

Living Sacrifices

Read the following situations and think of one way the person could imitate Jesus. Be ready to role-play the solution.

1 Tami's sister borrowed Tami's favorite sweater for picture day at school. As she was leaning against a locker talking to a friend, the sweater caught on a piece of metal. The sweater is ruined. Role-play the scene Tami has with her sister when she discovers the torn sweater.

2 Brandon's parents are divorced, so Brandon only sees his dad on weekends. When Brandon's dad picks him up after school on Friday, he tells Brandon that they will be spending the next day with his father's new girlfriend. Role-play the conversation Brandon has with his dad that night.

3 When Maria boards the school bus today, she notices her two best friends huddled over some papers. When she asks what they're doing, they say, "We've found a copy of the history test. Do you want the answers?" Maria did not study for this test. Role-play the conversation between Maria and her friends.

4 Toby and his buddies are playing basketball one day. The new kid from school rides up on his bike and watches the game. The teams are even, and they really don't need another player. Role-play the conversation between Toby and his buddies.

The Heroes in Your Family

Several years ago, the slogan was launched, "Christians aren't perfect, just forgiven." This message was plastered on signs, bumper stickers, and billboards. It's still somewhat popular today, and the message behind it is still powerful as well. The message is that we don't have to be perfect because we are forgiven for our imperfections. Because we are forgiven, we should strive to be perfect. It's a wonderful encouragement from God.

Applied to the topic of heroes, this slogan could be altered a bit: "Heroes aren't perfect, just used by God." The message is clear. God can and does use imperfect people for His perfect purposes. The Bible is full of people who were less than perfect spiritually, yet who were used by God to carry out His will. Abraham the liar, Jacob the thief, David the adulterer and murderer, Peter the denier, and Paul the persecutor all come to mind. It's important for heroes to realize that God uses imperfect people. Some are heroes in spite of their shortcomings (Abraham, Jacob, David), while some are not (Saul, Pilate). What is important, however, is that preteens understand that because people are not perfect, they need to be careful about whom they select as heroes. Likewise when heroes do make mistakes, preteens should note how these heroes handle their mistakes and what they do to overcome them. When heroes mess up, do they come back and set things right or do they continue to make the same mistakes? This question must be answered in order to determine if these heroes are still worthy of our admiration and honor.

Applied to the family, this topic is also crucial for preteens to understand. Like the heroes of our popular culture and of the Bible, parents and children are not perfect. Children may look up to their parents as heroes, and parents may consider some of the actions of their children as being heroic, but both will make mistakes at one time or another. What's important is how we, as a family, deal with those mistakes in order to make things right again.

In the following session, you will be given an opportunity to communicate this theme in a family setting. Because there are many types of families today (traditional, single-parent, blended), you will need to be sensitive to individual situations. The main issue here is to communicate to preteens that they must be careful in their choices of heroes, and that a determining factor in those choices is how those heroes handle their mistakes. Most importantly, you need to communicate that parents and children can still hold each other in high esteem after mistakes are made that may strain their relationships with each other. However, this can only happen if they take the proper steps to overcome these mistakes.

A "Chance" Encounter

Plan an overnight family camping trip for your group (a state park with camping facilities is ideal). Invite their parents in advance and get commitments from them to assist you with the planning and meals. For example, you may want to have "hero" sandwiches or other giant-sized foods to tie-in to the hero theme. When you arrive and set up your camping area, call everyone together for a brief time of introduction and explanation about the weekend. Have everyone introduce themselves so that people can get to know each other better. As part of these introductions, everyone must tell who they are and who their heroes are (parents must tell who their heroes were when they were children). Following introductions, inform everyone that the goals for the camping trip are to glorify God by examining their family relationships, and by becoming closer to the heroes in their own families.

Following this, say, "There are times in our family lives when we fail each other. Parents and kids both make mistakes. Sometimes this can cause us to lose respect for each other, but it doesn't always have to be that way." Ask the parents, "How do you feel when your kids fail you or willfully disobey you? This weekend we will examine some heroes in the Bible who failed, who willfully disobeyed God. Through their lives we will see if they continued to be heroes by overcoming their failures and mistakes. We will also examine our family lives this weekend. Although we may not want to admit it sometimes, we often look up to our parents as heroes. Likewise, your parents may look at you as heroes at times. It's important to remember that we all make mistakes. What really matters is what we do to overcome those mistakes. By overcoming them, we are truly heroes in our families."

Following this, have a time of singing and fellowship around the campfire. In case of rain, plan a video for the families to watch together in the central building. Some suggested titles include "Homeward Bound" and "Babe." Another movie that would fit well with the hero theme is "The Princess Bride." (Note: If you plan to use a video, you may want to preview it ahead of time to be sure it is appropriate for your group.) Be sure to have snacks and drinks to share. End the night with a group prayer, thanking God for the opportunity to be together, and asking Him to bless the rest of your time together.

Character Flaws

After waking up, eating breakfast, and cleaning up, tell everyone that they are going to play a game about popular heroes. Divide the group into two teams (do not split families in selecting teams). Tell everyone that they will be playing "Hero Charades." The object of the game is for a person to act out the actions of a popular hero who became famous for making a mistake at some point in their lives (suggested persons may be Magic Johnson, Pete Rose, Richard Nixon, Elvis Presley). If their team successfully guesses the hero you are acting out, then your team receives one point. The team with the most points wins; the team that loses must clean up after lunch.

After the game is played, inform everyone that you want to look at some heroes in the Bible who made mistakes or willfully sinned against God. Use copies of "Character Flaws" and Bibles. Divide the group into four smaller groups. Give each group on of the Scripture shields cut out from the reproducible page. Designate an area as the "hero" area. After the groups have finished answering their questions, have one person from each group act as the spokesperson. As you call the name of the first hero, the spokesperson from that group comes to the hero area and reports the groups answers. Continue this until all of the groups have reported their findings.

Materials
Bibles, photocopies of page 37

Family Time

Following the Bible study and discussion time, say, "We have seen some Bible heroes who made mistakes in their lives. Some repented and did what was necessary to make things right again. Some continued to make the same mistakes and do things their way. Those who chose to set things right can be considered heroes. It takes a big person to admit their faults. Those who continued in their mistakes are far from heroic."

Continue by saying, "In a few moments, you are going to get the chance to make things right with your family members. Take a walk through the woods with your family and talk to each other about your mistakes." Ask the parents, "How do you feel when your kids fail you or willfully disobey you?" Ask the kids, "How do you feel when your parents fail you?" Then ask both parents and children, "What do you do to make things right again? Be big enough to forgive one of your family members if they have failed or wronged you. If there are no unresolved issues in your family at this time, then take this time to express how much you love them, and how much of a hero they are to you." After this is done, return to the campsite for a wrap-up of the lesson and a time of prayer.

Wrap-Up

Close the weekend by saying, "You've seen that heroes are not perfect. You've seen some Bible heroes who messed up, and you know that even family members make mistakes at times. Be sure to honor the heroes in your family. When mistakes are made, talk about them and make things right. In this way, you are truly heroes, even when you're not perfect." Close with prayer. Give the group some free time for recreation or fellowship before lunch. After lunch, you can allow for more free time or make preparations to head back home. Before you leave, have a time of prayer in which each member of the group can participate. Focus on thanking God for their families and asking for wisdom in treating each other in a way that pleases Him.

Character Flaws

Samson

Read Judges 16:1-31.

1. What mistakes did Samson make?

2. Did Samson continue to disobey God, or did he make things right with Him?

3. Can Samson be considered a hero today? What can we learn from his life?

David

Read 2 Samuel 11:1-27; 12:1-14; Psalm 51:1-19.

1. What mistakes did David make?

2. Did he continue in his sin, or did he make things right with God? (see 2 Samuel 12:13)

3. What was David's attitude during this time? Was he truly sorry? (see Psalm 51)

4. Can David be considered a hero today? What can we learn from his life?

Peter

Read Matthew 26:69-75; John 21:1-19; Acts 2:14-40.

1. What mistakes did Peter make?

2. Did he continue in his mistake, or did he make things right with God?

3. How did God use Peter later in his life? (see Acts 2)

4. Can Peter be considered a hero today? What can we learn from his life?

Ananias & Sapphira

Read Acts 5:1-11.

1. What mistakes did Ananias and Sapphira make?

2. Did they make things right with God, or continue in their sins?

3. Can Ananias and Sapphira be considered heroes today? What can we learn from their lives?

Heroes Serving Heroes

We live in a world that promotes self and neglects others. Indeed many of us spend our entire lives in pursuit of self-gratification, and often we can never get enough. The idea of serving others without gaining anything in return is a lost one in today's society.

For children in the preteen years, this is often true as well. Influenced by the selfishness of their world, serving others is the last thing on their minds. Things can change, however. Preteens can realize that through serving others they become heroes to God and oftentimes to those whom they are serving. But that is not the major motivation for serving others. The main reason we serve others is that in doing so, we honor our Ultimate Hero—Jesus.

In this session, your preteens will get the opportunity to serve a group of people without receiving any reward. By planning and carrying out an event for children with special needs in their community, your students will come to understand that there is more to life than simply gratifying themselves. They will learn the blessings of reaching out to those in need. They will learn that in doing so, they are bringing glory to their Ultimate Hero—Jesus. Also, they will realize that God loves these children, and that He wants to express that love through their unselfishness.

God's Special Heroes

Your project will be to sponsor a picnic for children with special needs in your church or community. Several weeks prior to the picnic, you will need to contact the children's families and invite them to the picnic at a predetermined time and setting. If there are only a few children with special needs in your congregation, contact the social services department in your community and make your project known so the department can spread the word for you. Once you get commitments from your potential guests, you can begin preparations for the picnic.

Be sure to talk to the students beforehand to encourage them about the project. Encourage them not to look upon the children with fear. It's crucial that the students look beyond the physical appearances of these children, and look at them instead the way Jesus does—with unconditional love.

The theme for the picnic will be, "God's Special Heroes." The entire event will be divided into three major activities: games for the children to participate in, a lunch that your students will serve to the children, and an awards ceremony to honor the children. Games should be simple and achievable, yet challenging. Carnival-style games will work well. Younger children or children with severe physical disabilities may need some assistance from your students. Suggested games are listed below. Be sure your students encourage the children as they participate.

Game Time

Play some of these games.
Ring Toss (use plastic rings and empty two-liter soda bottles)
Bowling (use a plastic bowling set for children)
Basketball Free Throw Shooting
Clothes Basketball (a large Nerf ball and clothes basket)
Ball and Cans (use a tennis ball and coffee cans)

Following game time, serve a lunch of hot dogs and chips to the children. Again, encourage your students to help serve the food to the children. Following lunch, honor the children with "Medals of Honor" and tell them that they are heroes because of their perseverance and courage. Have your students design and make these medals beforehand and place them around the necks of the children during the ceremony. Close with a group prayer, thanking God for new friendships.

Project Review

After the picnic is over and everything is cleaned up, have the preteens meet together for a brief time of discussion that will focus on the project. Gather the students together and discuss the picnic. Ask, "How did it feel to help these children today? How do you think the children felt?" Say, "Let's take a few minutes and look at some people in the Bible who were physically challenged and see how Jesus related to them." Use the copies of "God's Special Heroes" with the discussion.

Following the discussion, say, "Jesus loved *all* people and helped them when He came in contact with them. Today you did the same thing when you sponsored the picnic for our friends. Jesus was a hero to the people He helped, and today you were heroes to the children because of your service to them." Read Philippians 2:3, 4 together and close with prayer, thanking God for the ability to serve others. Afterwards, take the group out to eat "hero" sandwiches.

Materials
photocopies of page 41

God's Special Heroes

Read Matthew 8:1-3.

1. What problem did the man want Jesus to help him with?
Why do you think he asked Jesus if He was willing to help him?

2. Jesus took a risk by touching the man. Do we take risks when we help people?

Read Mark 10:46-52.

1. The blind man cried out for help, but the world rejected him.
Are there times when the world rejects people with disabilities today?
Why do you think this happens?

2. Why do you think Jesus asked the man what he wanted Him to do?

Read Luke 13:10-13.

1. Jesus noticed the crippled lady before she noticed Him.
What can we do to have a better awareness of those who need help today?

2. How do we help "set people free" when we reach out to help them today?

Read John 5:1-9.

1. Why would Jesus ask the man if he wanted to get well?
Would Jesus have healed him if he said "no"?

2. How do you think the lame man felt after Jesus healed him?
How did he feel about Jesus?

Unit 2
Servant Quest

Be Your Own Hero

The first unit in this book was designed to guide your preteens in their selections of heroes. In this unit, we will take that idea one step further. Servant Quest encourages your preteens to become heroes themselves by actively serving God and others. Help preteens build an attitude of service.

Many times adults speak to preteens in terms of the future. Teachers may tell them, "Study now so you'll be successful when you're an adult." Parents my say, "When you're older you can stay out later." Although these statements are true, they may be frustrating to preteens. They begin to believe that life really starts after they grow up. This unit is designed to let preteens know that they don't have to wait until they are adults to serve the Lord. They can serve Him right now!

Each session in this unit provides activities and suggestions your preteens can utilize to prepare them in service.

Bridge the Gap

This session unites preteens and their parents. To carry out the theme of service, families plan a recycling program for their church. By helping to conserve and recycle everyday

Session 1—
Standard of Service Is Jesus
Know that Jesus served others and glorified God.
Feel a desire to follow Jesus' example and glorify God by serving others.
Identify ways to serve and glorify God.

Session 2—
Caring for Others
Know that acts of kindness done for others are also done to Jesus.
Feel confident that God accepts our service to others as love for Him and His Son.
Contrast reasons for serving others that might be done for Jesus with selfish choices that disregard Him.

Session 3—
Develop Skills That Can Help Others
Know that people can serve God best by using the gifts He provides.
Feel confidence in doing things well.
Identify ways each person can serve God best.

Session 4—
Build Teams That Will Serve
Know that a Christian team works together, building up other members and doing acts of service that glorify God.
Feel the desire to be a part of a team for Christ.
Identify skills to use in teamwork.

items, these families can help to keep God's earth clean while possibly providing extra money to donate to mission projects.

Go to Extremes

At the end of each session, students will be working on a service mobile. This mobile represents acts of service the preteens will do during the week.

The students can display these mobiles at a party for senior adults. During Session 2, students are encouraged to organize a club that provides services to these senior saints. The party will allow both groups to meet and encourage one another.

Daily Devotions

The following Scriptures are provided for you and your students as you study this unit. Read and encourage your students to read one Scripture each day.

Week 1	Week 2	Week 3	Week 4
Standard of Service Is Jesus	**Caring for Others**	**Develop Skills That Can Help Others**	**Build Teams That Will Serve**
Finding our strength and perseverance in God.	Finding comfort in knowing God cares for us.	Doing what God has called us to do.	Living as Christians in our actions and attitudes.
Monday 2 Timothy 1:7	**Monday** Proverbs 15:3	**Monday** James 1:22	**Monday** Romans 12:9-12
Tuesday Hebrews 12:2, 3	**Tuesday** Psalm 33:13-15	**Tuesday** 1 Timothy 6:12	**Tuesday** Galatians 5:22
Wednesday Proverbs 3:5, 6	**Wednesday** Isaiah 41:10	**Wednesday** Isaiah 40:28-31	**Wednesday** Ecclesiastes 5:2, 3
Thursday Mark 12:30	**Thursday** Psalm 23	**Thursday** Ephesians 2:10	**Thursday** Philippians 2:1-11
Friday Philippians 4:13	**Friday** Matthew 7:7, 8	**Friday** Romans 12:1, 2	**Friday** 1 Corinthians 15:58
Saturday Ecclesiastes 7:13, 14	**Saturday** Galatians 10:13	**Saturday** 1 Corinthians 12:4-6	**Saturday** Matthew 6:19-24
Sunday Ephesians 6:13-18	**Sunday** Psalm 18:1-3	**Sunday** Romans 12:6-8	**Sunday** 1 Corinthians 13

Standard of Service Is Jesus

Scripture. Matthew 6:1-4; Philippians 2:5; Colossians 3:17

Know that Jesus served others and glorified God.

Feel a desire to follow Jesus' example and glorify God by serving others.

Identify ways to serve and glorify God.

Get Into the Game

To begin this session, the students will be playing a Pictionary game with occupations as clues. Prior to the session, write the following occupations on slips of paper: actor, butler, chauffeur, doctor, gardener, lawyer, maid, minister, missionary, nurse, opera singer, teacher.

Divide the class into two teams. Each team will take turns drawing a slip of paper and guessing an occupation. Allow one minute for each guess.

After all of the clues have been guessed, ask the students, "Of all the occupations mentioned in this game, which ones would you consider to be service-type jobs?" (butler, chauffeur, gardener, maid, possibly even minister, missionary, and nurse)

"What's the difference between service jobs and the other jobs mentioned?" (service jobs pay less; society views them as menial jobs; usually involve working for someone else; nonglamorous)

Next have the students think of people in the Bible that they would consider to be servants of God. Record the names on the board as the students give them. People such as Abraham, Noah, Moses, David, the disciples, Mary and Martha, and Paul are just a few of the many that can be used. You may want to give them some of these names to get them started. Encourage them to think of as many names as they can on their own. Ask the students what these people did to be considered servants of God. Try to find a reason for each of the people listed. The students may simply identify the story associated with each person.

Materials
chalk and a chalkboard or drawing easel with paper and markers, watch with second hand or some kind of timer, slips of paper with occupations written on them

Step 1

Have students turn to Philippians 2:5-11 in their Bibles and have a volunteer read the passage.

This Scripture tells us exactly how to be a servant and gives us an example of a true servant. Ask the following questions:

1. What is an attitude? (What you are thinking or telling yourself when you are doing something.)

2. Whose attitude should ours be like?" (Jesus Christ)

3. When Jesus became human what did He take the nature or form of? (a servant)

Remind students that although Jesus could have saved himself from death on the cross, He suffered and died to accomplish a much greater mission.

Now have students read James 4:10 and Matthew 6:1. To be an effective servant, one must be humble and take direction from others. Ask students to define the word *humble* (not proud; not thinking too highly of oneself). Remind students that God rewards those with a humble attitude.

Have students read 1 Corinthians 10:31. Have students think of the ways people give God glory for what they do (thank Him; give a tithe or offering). Remind students that although they may be performing the service, God still should receive the glory.

Distribute photocopies of "Servant for Hire!" Have students write job descriptions that will be advertisements for service. The descriptions should include the information they have just learned about God's requirements for being a servant. For example: "At your service, a young, able-bodied servant. Hard worker and eager to please. Ready to give God all the glory for my abilities." If the students need help, you may want to use telephone or newspaper ads as examples. When the students are finished, have each of them read their ads. Collect the ads and save them to use as a bulletin board display.

Materials

photocopies of page 47, markers or crayons, telephone or newspaper classified ads (optional)

Step 2

Have students read Colossians 3:17. Remind them that no matter what occupation a person has, there is always a way to be a servant for God. Distribute copies of "How Can I Serve?" Divide the class into the teams used earlier in the Pictionary game. Have the teams look at the occupations symbolized on the sheet. The team members should work together to list ways these occupations can serve God. For example:

1. actor—perform dramas for the worship service

2. doctor/nurse—volunteer services on short-term mission trips

Materials

photocopies of page 48

3. cook/chef—volunteer time at drop-in or homeless shelters to cook meals

4. singer/musician—take part in worship services

5. carpenter/plumber—repair church building or a mission

6. writer—help with the church newspaper; write notes to the sick and shut-ins

7. artist—help paint church building or design signs and banners for the worship area

8. teacher—teach Sunday school or VBS

After teams have finished, let each group report their results. Remind students that many people in the Bible had a trade or job, but they still found time to serve the Lord.

Step 3

Read Matthew 6:1-4. Divide the class into three groups. Each group will develop and perform a scenario that portrays service in one of three areas: friendship, school, home, and/or family. Encourage the groups to think of ways to serve God "silently" in these three areas. After the groups have developed their skits, have them perform the skits for the rest of the class. When all of the skits have been performed, remind the students that they can serve God at any age.

Take It to the Next Level

At the end of each session in this unit, students will be working on a service mobile that will be displayed during a special worship service during the **Go to Extremes** session. For the next three weeks, the students must perform at least one act of service between sessions. At the end of each session, the students will add that act of service to their mobiles. If the students need suggestions, they could help a friend at school, do something helpful for their parents, distribute bulletins at the next worship service, or anything else they can think of.

This week, allow the students to cover the center of the hanger. They should take two pieces of construction paper and trace the shield pattern (page 72) onto them. Cut the shields out of the paper, then write the following on both sides: "I will serve God by . . ." Have the students staple the shields together. The construction paper should now cover the center of the hanger, but still allow room at the bottom of the hanger to tie yarn onto later.

Remind students to perform at least one act of service this week so they can add it to their mobiles next week. Close the session with prayer.

Materials
wire clothes hangers (one per student), construction paper, markers, scissors, pencils, photocopies of page 72, staplers

Servant for Hire!

Create an advertisement that will convince others you are qualified to be a servant.

How Can I Serve?

These pictures symbolize various occupations.
Next to the symbols, write ways that people in these occupations can serve God.

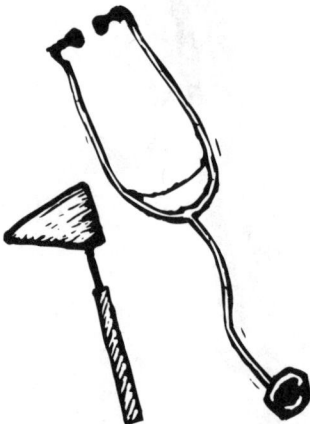

Caring for Others

Scripture. Matthew 25:34-40

Know that acts of kindness done for others are also done to Jesus.

Feel confident that God accepts our service to others as love for Him and His Son.

Contrast reasons for serving others that might be done for Jesus with selfish choices that disregard Him.

Get Into the Game

For this charade activity you will need to divide the class into six groups. (Option: If you have fewer than twelve students, use three or four groups and give more than one letter to each group.) Write the letters of the word *caring* on small pieces of paper. Each of the groups will be given one letter of the word and decide on an activity beginning with their letter that would represent caring for someone.

After agreeing on the activity, each group helps one person or several people act it out for the rest of the class.

Some possibilities are:

C—cleaning, cooperating, carrying
A—arranging, applauding
R—rescuing, reading
I—including, initiating
N—being neighborly, being nice
G—giving, guarding

Answer any questions that the students may have as you randomly distribute the letters to each of the groups.

Give them several minutes to work on their charades.

Try to put as much distance between the groups as possible. This will help keep the activities confidential.

Have each group do their charades and allow the other groups to guess.

Materials

each letter from the word *caring* written on small slips of paper

Step 1

Gather the students back into one large group. Have them find Matthew 25:34-40 in their Bibles. Tell the students, "This Scripture gives us the reason to care for others." Have students take turns reading each verse from this passage. When the passage has been read, ask, "Who is the King in this story?" (Jesus) "When did Jesus say they had helped Him?" (When He

Materials

photocopies of page 52

was hungry, thirsty, a stranger, needing clothes, sick, in prison) "Who else was being helped in all of the situations?" (Jesus) Remind students that each time we help someone, we are helping and pleasing God.

Distribute photocopies of "Attitude Check!" and pencils. Students will be rating themselves on each statement given. Encourage the students to work individually. This is a time for each student to evaluate his attitude about caring.

After the students have finished, tell them they will be working in teams for the next activity.

Step 2

Distribute photocopies of "The Great Scavenger Hunt." Divide the students into two teams. The teams will be competing in a scavenger hunt to find items that can be used in service. Each team should choose one person to be the designated recorder for that team. The recorder will stay in the room or "headquarters" to record the findings. Each time a team finds an item pictured on the sheet, they must bring it back for the recorder to cross off the page. Groups can bring only one item at a time. They do not have to find the items in the order given.

Before the teams begin say, "In the last activity, we discussed giving God the glory when we care for others. Now we will discover what we can use when we care for others."

Explain the rules of the scavenger hunt. Determine the boundaries for the hunt and set a time limit. You may want to give small prizes to the team that finds the most items.

After everyone has returned, have the teams take turns choosing one item and describing how it could be used to care for someone. Some possible answers include:
1. Dollar bill—give to a mission project.
2. Gift—give to a secret pal.
3. Trash bag—use to collect toys for needy kids.
4. Aluminum can—donate to a food pantry.
5. Hammer—use to help build a Habitat for Humanity house.
6. Pen—write a note to someone who is sick or grieving.
7. Spoon—use to feed a hungry child or give medicine to a sick person.
8. Cleaning sponge—use to help clean the church building.
9. Band-Aid—cover a child's scraped knee while volunteering in VBS.
10. Hymnal—use to sing for shut-ins in a nursing home.

Materials
photocopies of page 53, two of each item listed on the reproducible page to hide in a pre-determined area, small prizes (optional)

Step 3

In this activity, students will organize a club for the purpose of helping others. The main target group for this activity should be the older people in the church. The students will need to define the type of activities this club could do, as well as come up with a name for the club. Say to the students, "There are many things we can do to help care for others in the church—especially the older people. If we formed a special club to help the older people in our church, what types of things do you think we could do for them?" Let the students discuss.

Conclude that one way to know what to do would be to ask. Have the students suggest ways they could gather information from the older people. Guide them to include request boxes in their ideas.

Spend some time having the students make request boxes by decorating shoe boxes. When the students have decorated the boxes, have them place the boxes around the church and in the Sunday school classrooms of the older adults so that people will be able to place their requests in them. You may also want to have the students make short announcements to the classes introducing the club and themselves. There will need to be one person that will be responsible for checking the boxes for the requests. Each time the group meets, they will discuss how they can meet the request that has been asked of the club. This can be a long-term activity that will help encourage communication and relationships within the church.

Take It to the Next Level

Before closing the session, have students work on their mobiles. Ask the students, "How many remembered to do at least one act of service this week? What did you do?" Allow students the opportunity to respond. Then have them choose and trace one shape from page 73 onto a piece of construction paper. They should write the act of service they performed on both sides of the shape, leaving space at the top for the hole punch. Then have students tie a piece of yarn one to two inches long through the hole and attach it to the bottom of the hanger. Remind students to help in a different way each week. They can add their actions to their mobiles next week. Close the session with prayer.

Attitude ✔Check!

Read the following statements and fill in the number for each statement that most closely matches your attitude. Total your score at the bottom.

1—No way!   **2—Only if I have to!**   **3—That's me!**

_____ 1. I leave my Sunday school class just as I find it.

_____ 2. I clean my room without being asked.

_____ 3. I go out of my way to make new kids feel welcome.

_____ 4. I would give up something I own for someone who needs it more than I do.

_____ 5. I would get up early on Saturday to volunteer in my community.

_____ 6. I never talk during a church service.

_____ 7. I would spend time with the elderly and visit retirement homes.

_____ 8. I would spend time with a mentally or physically challenged person.

_____ 9. I would run errands for a sick neighbor.

_____ 10. I would work hard to earn enough money for a missionary.

✔   ✔   ✔   ✔   ✔

My total was _____.

25-30—You are a very caring person! You have a great attitude when it comes to helping others. Keep up the good work!

20-24—You care most of the time, but it doesn't come naturally. You may need to work on your attitude.

15-19—You need to check your attitude. Remember Matthew 25:40 and work on being a caring person.

"I tell you the truth, whatever you did for one of the least of these brothers of mine, you did for me"
(Matthew 25:40, NIV).

THE GREAT SCAVENGER HUNT

Find the following items and bring them to your group's recorder.

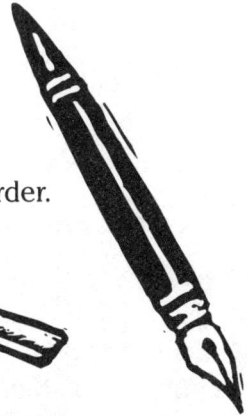

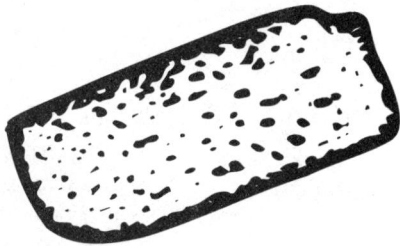

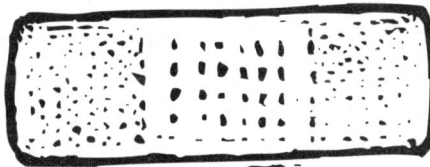

Develop Skills That Can Help Others

Scripture. 1 Corinthians 12:4-6; Ephesians 2:10; James 1:17; 1 Peter 4:10

Know that people can serve God best by using the gifts He provides.
Feel confidence in doing things well.
Identify ways each person can serve God best.

Get Into the Game

This relay will get the students excited about the session, but also give them a chance to understand that people have different talents and gifts. Divide the class into two groups with an even number of students in each group. If you have an odd number of students, appoint one student as judge.

Each group will need their own course set up. Arrange the relay courses so there will be enough room for four stopping points. Use chairs to designate stopping points. Depending on the amount of space you have, you can decide whether or not to place the chairs in a straight line or to vary the direction of the course.

Tape instructions (cut from page 58) at each chair. At each stopping point, students will be required to read instructions and do the skill that you have taped there. Place a finish line at the end of each course with masking tape or ribbon. The next person in the group begins the course when the previous student crosses the finish line.

Tell the students, "We are going to have a relay race. In this race, each chair will be a stopping point. You will need to read the directions found at each stop. After you complete the task, you may go on to the next stop. The group to have all of its members cross the finish line first wins."

The stops should be set up as follows:

Stop #1—Find 1 Peter 4:10 and read it aloud.

Stop #2—Complete five jumping jacks; then touch your toes.

Stop #3—Sing "Jesus Loves Me."

Stop #4—Jump rope while shouting compliments such as "Awesome!" and "Good job!"

Tell the students, "When the person in front of you crosses

Materials

eight folding chairs, photocopy of page 58, pen, masking tape or ribbon, two Bibles, two jump ropes over the finish line, the next person in the group may begin. Be sure not to start until they have crossed the line. Are there any questions?"

Answer any questions the students may have. Give the students the signal to begin the race. Watch carefully to make sure that all the racers are completing the activity at each stopping point. The student judge, if you appointed one, can help.

When all of the students have finished, ask the following questions:

"Did you find that some of the tasks at the stopping points were harder for you than the other tasks? Why?"

Encourage students to give their explanations. Make the point that not everyone has the same talents or gifts.

Step 1

Have the students find and read the following Bible verses:
1 Peter 4:10; Ephesians 2:10; James 1:17; 1 Corinthians 12:4-6, 11.

After the Scriptures have been read, ask the students the following questions.

1. What should we do with our gifts? (1 Peter 4:10)

2. Where do our gifts come from? (James 1:17)

3. Explain 1 Corinthians 12:4-6, 11. (No matter what gift you have, it comes from God and should be used to glorify God.)

After students have answered the questions, divide them into groups of four to six members. Provide a variety of small boxes and containers. (Plastic Easter eggs could also be used as containers.) You will also need gift wrap or blank newsprint and several rolls of tape. Give students photocopies of "Everyone Is Special!" and pencils. Instruct the students to cut the paper into the sections indicated. Each group member needs a slip of paper for every other group member. It might be best to keep boys and girls in separate groups. Have each student write down one special thing about every person in the group. Students should then place each piece of paper in a container and wrap it as if it were a gift, using a name tag with each gift. Give students plenty of time to write and wrap each present.

Materials
photocopies of page 59, scissors, small boxes or containers, tape, wrapping paper

Step 2

In this activity the students will identify how every person is unique and special. The students will be drawing silhouettes of their profiles on white construction paper. You need a bright light source to create a distinct silhouette. A lamp or overhead projector would work well for this. Make a silhouette of yourself before class time to show them how it will look when it is finished.

Materials
white and colored construction paper, pencils, scissors, markers, overhead projector or lamp, tape, glue sticks, ink pad

Have each student tape a piece of white construction paper on the wall. The student will face the paper while the light shines behind him. As the light shines, the student should trace his outline on the paper. (Note: If the student would prefer a profile, someone else will have to trace the image for him.)

After the students have taken turns in front of the light, they will then cut out their profiles. Now glue the silhouettes on larger pieces of colored construction paper. The students may also add thumbprints to the colored construction paper next to their silhouette. They can compare thumbprints with each other to reinforce the idea that although we may look similar and do things in a similar way, we are all different. God loved us enough to take the time to create each of us as a unique person.

Say to the students, "When God created us, He made mankind so that no two people have ever been alike. Even identical twins have differences between them. Each one of us has our own unique talents and skills to go along with our appearance. What I would like for you to do now is think of the gifts that God has given you and write them on your silhouette." Write several things on your silhouette as examples. Distribute gift boxes. When they are finished, allow them to exchange their presents. Every student should have several gifts to open.

When they have had the opportunity to unwrap and read their gifts, ask the student, "Did you know that you had these gifts and talents before you were given the presents? Does it help when other people point out talents and gifts to us?" Let the students respond to the questions. You may ask some of the students for examples to demonstrate their response.

Ask if any of the students would like to share their finished project with the rest of the group. Do not force any students to share. Some of the students may have written some personal talents they may feel uncomfortable sharing. However, sharing your own silhouette may help encourage the students.

Step 3

Distribute photocopies of "Talent Search." Have students read the descriptions given and write at least one talent each person might be good at and one they might not be good at.

After students have finished the activity, say, "Each one of us has been made in the image of God. We all have gifts or talents that we are good at, but we probably won't be good at everything. When we can accept our strengths and weaknesses, then when can accept others for their unique gifts." Go over the activity with the students. Some possible answers include:

Materials
photocopies of page 60

1. Toby could help plan games and activities for an after-school program for kids. Since he doesn't like to sit still, he probably wouldn't be good at tutoring.

2. Maria would probably be good working with small children. She probably wouldn't be good leading a choir.

3. Cassandra could make baked goods for shut-ins and deliver them to nursing or retirement homes. She might not be as good in her school's peer counseling program.

4. Nick could help tutor or volunteer in the church office. He might not be good on the church softball team.

5. Brittany could tape-record herself reading books and magazines for the visually impaired. She might not be good at mentoring or counseling.

6. Matthew would be great in a worship band or accompanying a choir. He might not be as good on the Bible Bowl team.

Take It to the Next Level

Before closing the session, have students work on their mobiles. Ask the students, "How many of you remembered to do another act of service this week? What did you do?" Allow students the opportunity to respond. Then have them choose and trace one of the shapes from page 73 onto construction paper. Cut out the shape and write the act of service they performed on both sides of the shape, leaving space at the top for the hole punch. Then have students tie a piece of yarn one to two inches long through the hole and attach it to the bottom of the hanger. Remind students to perform a different act of service this week. They can add it to their mobiles next week. Close the session with prayer.

Materials
hanger mobiles, photocopies of page 73, construction paper, scissors, yarn, markers, hole punch

Stop 1 **Find 1 Peter 4:10 and read it aloud.**	**Stop 1** **Find 1 Peter 4:10 and read it aloud.**
Stop 2 Complete five jumping jacks; then touch your toes.	**Stop 2** Complete five jumping jacks; then touch your toes.
Stop 3 Sing, "Jesus Loves Me."	**Stop 3** Sing, "Jesus Loves Me."
Stop 4 Jump rope while shouting compliments such as "Awesome!" and "Good Job!"	**Stop 4** Jump rope while shouting compliments such as "Awesome!" and "Good Job!"

Everyone Is Special!

Write something special about each person in your group. What talents do they use for others? Cut the slips of paper apart. Put each paper in a box. Wrap and put gift tags on the boxes to give to your group members.

_____

is special because

_____
_____
_____

_____

is special because

_____
_____
_____

_____

is special because

_____
_____
_____

_____

is special because

_____
_____
_____

To: _____

To: _____

To: _____

To: _____

Talent Search

Read the following descriptions and write one talent or gift each person might have and one ability that person might not be good at.

_____

1 Toby is very tall for his age. He is a good runner, and he likes to move around a lot. He has trouble sitting still for long periods of time.

2 Maria is very shy and quiet. She doesn't like to talk a lot, but she is a very good listener.

3 Cassandra loves to help her mom in the kitchen. In fact, she'd much rather spend time with adults than with her peers.

4 Nick spends hours alone at his computer. He can work any computer program.

5 Brittany loves to talk. Sometimes her talking gets her into trouble at school.

6 Matthew is an excellent guitar player. He can memorize almost any piece of music, but he has trouble memorizing facts.

Session 4

Build Teams That Will Serve

Scripture. Romans 12:4, 5; 15: 5, 6; 1 Corinthians 12:12, 27

Know that a Christian team works together, building up other members and doing acts of service that glorify God.

Feel the desire to be a part of a team for Christ.

Identify skills to use in teamwork.

Get Into the Game

You will need open floor space for this activity. Have students spell the word *teamwork* one letter at a time working together to making the shape of the letters as fast as they can. When you say the letter *T,* all of the students will work together to make one large *T.* Use a stop watch to time their progress. Challenge them to do it faster each time. Doing it as a race against time adds to the fun.

Say, "I am going to see how well you work as a team. You are going spell the word *teamwork* with your bodies."

Give them one letter at a time. Tell them how many seconds it took to make the letters as you work your way through the word. Challenge them to form the next letter quicker. When they finish this activity, they may need a few moments to settle down before they begin the next activity.

Step 1

Have the students take their Bibles and look up Romans 12:4, 5; 15:5, 6; 1 Corinthians 12:12, 27. Distribute photocopies of "God's Team" and pencils. After the students have read the Scripture, have them each answer the questions on the sheet. When the students have finished, go over the questions together.

Materials
photocopies of page 64

1. What do all of us together make? (one body—Romans 12:4, 5)
2. What does God give us? (endurance, encouragement, spirit of unity—Romans 15:5, 6)
3. What are we to do with our mouths? (glorify God)
4. What do all the parts of the body make? (a unit—1 Corinthians 12:12, 27)
5. In 1 Corinthians 12:12, 27, who is the body? (Christ)

The next few activities are going to give the students practice working together as teams to accomplish a goal.

Step 2

The purpose of this activity is to show that the members of a team use different talents and abilities. We must learn how to work together regardless of the combinations of team members' talents or abilities to get the task accomplished. The students will need to be divided into groups of three for this activity. The groups of three will be making a map from the church parking lot to the home of one of the three.

However, this is where the activity becomes a challenge. One of the three will not be able to speak. This person should have tape over his mouth. Another person will not be able to see. This person should be blindfolded. The other person in the group will not be able to use his hands. You could tie his arms next to his body. Be careful not to injure any one with these modifications. Provide adult supervision for each group, if necessary.

Each group must decide what each person's role will be (unable to speak, unable to see, or unable to use their hands). Who will be drawing the map? Whose house will be mapped out?

Remind the groups that each person must contribute to the mapmaking process in some way. They may use any landmarks or street names they choose, while trying to be as accurate as possible.

Answer any questions that the students may have. Distribute the blindfolds, tape, and string to the students. Help any of the groups that need assistance in getting ready. Signal the groups to begin. Give the groups several minutes to work on their maps. Encourage students to be creative in their efforts to communicate. When time is up, give students the opportunity to show their work and explain how they worked together. Ask the following questions:

1. How did you compensate for the problems?
2. How did each person's talents help the group?
3. How did you overcome discouragement and frustration?

Materials
blindfolds, tape, string

Step 3

Students will trace one part of each person's body to create one group "body." For example, one person could trace a hand, another an arm, another a head, and so forth. Once the body parts are traced, cut the parts out.

Then, students should write ideas for a service project on each body part. Some ideas include:

1. Plan a program for a retirement or nursing home.
2. Choose a Saturday to do yard work or housework for church members.

Materials
scissors, butcher paper, tape, photocopies of page 65

3. Prepare a newsletter with photos to send to missionary families.

4. Plan and carry out a work day at the church.

After students have brainstormed ideas, have them tape the body parts together. Students should then decide which activity they would like to do. Distribute photocopies of "Body Building" to help them in their planning of the activity. Encourage the students to set a time to carry out the activity.

Take It to the Next Level

Before closing the session, have students work to complete their mobiles. Ask the students, "How many of you performed another act of service this week? What did you do?" Allow students the opportunity to respond. Then have them choose and trace one shape from page 73 onto construction paper and cut it out. They should write the act of service they performed on both sides of the shape, leaving space at the top for the hole punch. Then have students tie a piece of yarn one to two inches long through the hole and attach it to the bottom of the hanger. The mobiles are now complete, and the students may take them home this week. Encourage students to continue doing acts of service. Close the session with prayer.

Materials
hanger mobiles, photocopies of page 73, construction paper, scissors, yarn, markers, hole punch

We're All Part of God's Team

Read Romans 12:4, 5; 15:5, 6; and 1 Corinthians 12:27.
Answer the following questions.

Romans 12:4, 5	Romans 15:5, 6	1 Corinthians 12:12, 27

1 What do all of us together make?

2 What does God give us?

3 What are we to do with our mouths?

4 What do all the parts of the body make?

5 Who is the body?

Body Building

What can we do to build up the "body of Christ" in our church?

Use the following questions to help you decide.

5. When will we do this activity?

4. Will we need money? If so, how much? Where will we get it?

3. What will we need?

1. What will we do?

2. Who will help us?

Caring for Creation

God has given us a responsibility to take care of His earth. This session is designed to unite families in organizing and planning a recycling program or event for their church.

Before you begin, prepare by doing the following:

1. Contact any recycling centers in your area. Find out what types of items they accept (plastic, glass, aluminum, newspaper). Ask if they will pay for any donations and if there are any special requirements to be fulfilled before donating (i.e., washing any cans or bottle, removing labels, crushing items, etc.).

2. Contact your church leaders about starting a recycling center at the church. Ask if you can set containers in designated areas over an extended period of time. If not, plan one day to collect all of the items.

After you have obtained the necessary information, you can plan the event. There are several options for you to choose from depending on your resources. Use one or all of the ideas given with your group. Choose whatever works best for the needs of your group and church.

Clean up the Neighborhood

Plan a day for families to meet at the church. Tell them to wear old clothes and bring gloves. Supply trash bags.

Once everyone has arrived, have the families work together to comb the area in your town or city and pick up any trash or recyclable items. Be sure to put all the trash in one bag and any recyclable item in a separate bag.

Set a time for the families to return to the church. At this time they can dispose of the trash they have collected and sort through any recyclable items. When all of the items have been sorted and the families have washed their hands, provide a lunch of "leftovers" or "green" items to represent environmental friendliness (i.e., salads, white grapes, lime jello, etc.).

Recycling Drive

Several weeks in advance, have families get together to plan an all-church recycling drive. Photocopy the poster (page 68) to make signs to hang in the church hallways. Have the families trace the lettering onto posterboard or color the photocopies with bright markers. Set a date and time for the drive. Display the signs throughout the church.

You may want to contact people in the church that own pickup trucks to help you with the drive. Once the day has been set, assign each family a duty. One family could be in charge of glass bottles, another could be in charge of newspapers, and so forth.

When the day arrives, supply garbage bags for families to put the recyclables in. When everything has been collected, deliver it to the recycling center. If any money is collected from the drive, be sure to donate it to the church building and grounds budget or to the missions budget.

Clothing Drive

Plan a day to collect gently used clothing to be donated to a thrift store or homeless shelter in your area.

Photocopy the poster (page 69) and put these signs throughout your church. Put a note in your church newspaper informing people of the clothing drive. Designate a day for the clothes to be taken to the church, or set boxes and large containers throughout the church to collect the items over several weeks.

Once the clothing has been collected, have the families sort through the items. Tell them to separate the clothing into the following categories: men's, women's, boy's, girl's, and baby clothes. Once the items have been sorted, put them in marked bags or boxes and deliver them to the thrift store or shelter.

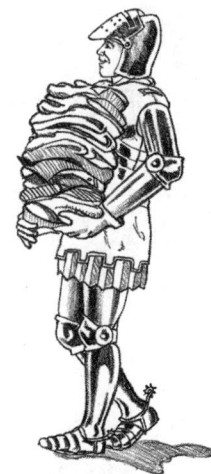

All-Church Recycling Day

Date:

Time:

What to bring:

All-Church Clothing Drive

Date:

Time:

What to Bring:

All items will be donated to:

Go to Extremes

Celebrating Senior Saints

This session builds upon ideas introduced in Session 2. During this session, students were to start a club that provided help and services to the senior adults in the church.

This session is an opportunity for your preteens to meet these people and thank them for their years of service.

Plan a party and invite the older adults. Select a day, time, and place for the party. Be sure to get this approved by your church leaders. Photocopy the art on page 74 and have students make invitations. Have the church office mail them, or have your preteens hand deliver them during Sunday school.

Photocopy page 75 for your students. Have them decorate the certificates with bright colors, stickers, or glitter. Make sure they fill in a name on each certificate. The students will present these certificates during the party.

In advance, decorate the room with balloons, streamers, and a banner that says, "Thank You, Senior Servants!" Have the students provide food for the party. You can make the menu simple by providing snack foods such as cheese and crackers, fruit, and cookies, or if your group is adventurous, have them

Materials
photocopies of pages 74 and 75

70

plan a whole meal.

Once the seniors arrive, have the students help to serve the food and beverages. Make sure the seniors feel pampered by your preteens.

In advance, have students record themselves singing some choruses or hymns. While the seniors are visiting, play the recording as background music.

When the adults have finished eating, plan a short program. In advance, have students prepare to tell the seniors what they have been studying during this unit. Have them present their service mobiles and tell the adults what they have accomplished. Then have them give each person present a certificate they have made that praises the seniors for their service. Close the session with prayer.

Service Mobile

Cut this shield out and trace it onto two pieces of construction paper.
Assemble the pieces together
as directed in each session.

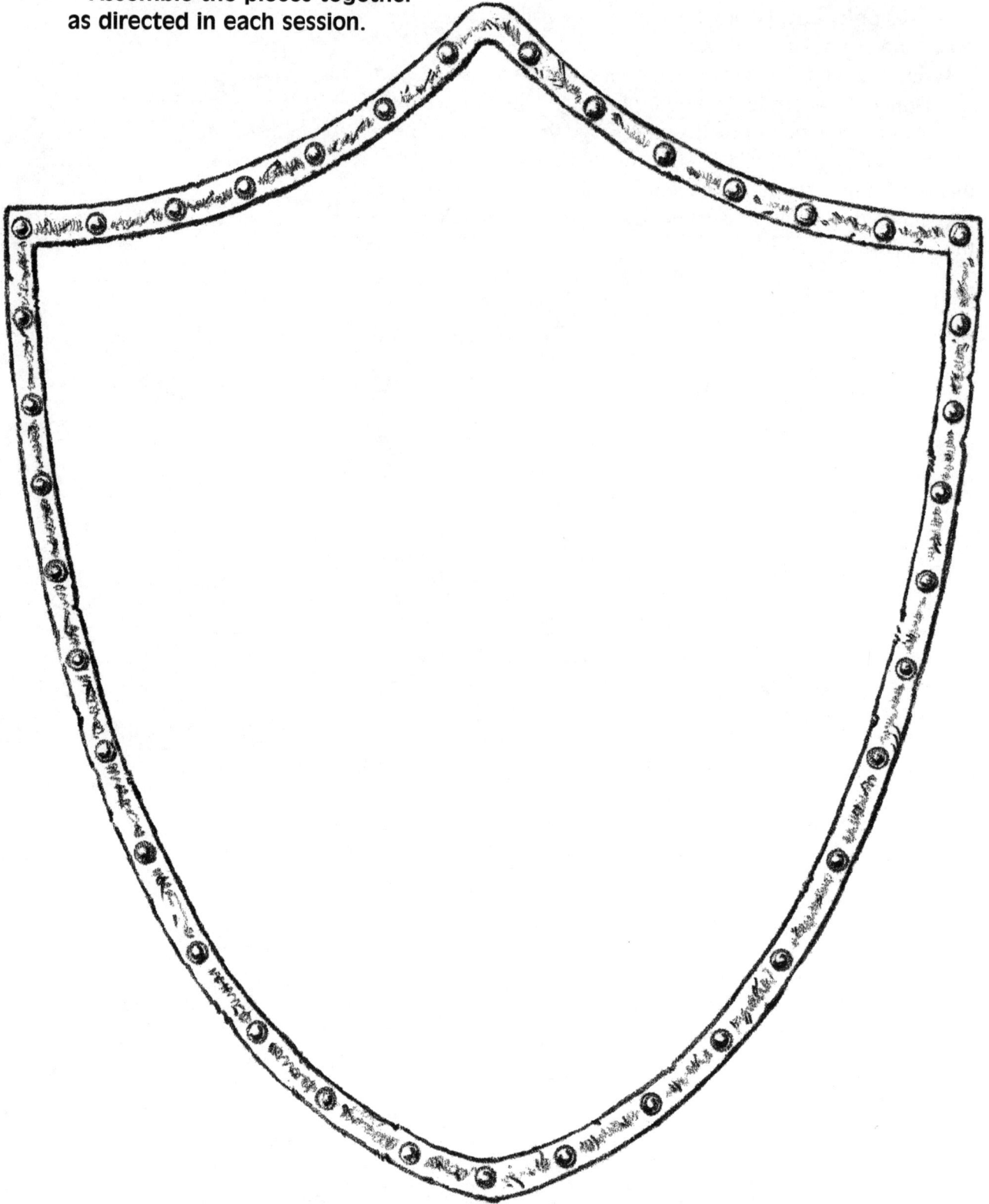

Service Mobile

Cut out one shape each week,
glue it to construction paper,
and cut it out again.

Assemble the pieces as directed
in each session to make a mobile.

You're Invited!

Who:

When:

Where:

In Appreciation

This certificate signifies that

has provided time and talents
to the glory of God!

Character Quest

Heroes: People of Faith

Where do preteens find their heroes? Most find them from TV and movie actors, sports personalities, and recording artists. Are these the role models we want our preteens to emulate? This unit is designed to offer some alternatives and introduce students to heroes from the Bible. These men and women were ordinary people that God used for extraordinary purposes. Through study of these heroes, preteens will learn that God can use any of us for extraordinary purposes. Students will understand that God can empower them as He empowered the Bible heroes. Students will see God's mercy and grace as God used people who were not perfect and made mistakes.

A dual purpose of this unit is to help preteens learn about Bible chronology. Even in churches, many children, youth, and adults are not knowledgeable about the Bible. This lack of knowledge will result in persons looking elsewhere than to God and His Word for help, comfort, authority, and direction. This unit uses selected Bible characters to teach Bible chronology. As we encourage preteens to learn about the Bible, they will see its relevance to their lives.

As a knowledge-based unit, much information is communicated to students to help them learn about these heroes and

Session 1—
Heroes Have Faith in God
Aim. Students learn that God used these Bible heroes because they had faith in Him.

Heroes. Adam, Eve, Abel, Noah, Abraham, Sarah, Isaac, Jacob, Joseph, Miriam, Moses, Rahab, Joshua

Session 2—
Heroes Obey God
Aim. Students learn that when Israelite heroes obey God, their nation prospers and is kept safe. When they disobey, sin reigns and the Israelites suffer.

Heroes. Deborah, Gideon, Samson, Ruth, Hannah, Samuel, Saul, David, Solomon

Session 3—
Heroes Are Faithful Through Trials
Aim. Students learn there may be special trials in this world as a result of their commitment to God, but God is faithful. He will help them persevere.

Heroes. Elijah, Jonah, Isaiah, Daniel, Esther, Nehemiah

Session 4—
Heroes Tell Others About Jesus
Aim. Students will understand that the New Testament heroes lived and proclaimed their faith in Christ, even when those actions endangered their lives.

Heroes. John the Baptist, Nicodemus, Peter, Matthew, Mary Magdalene, Stephen, Paul, Priscilla

76

their place in Bible history. To discover stories about most Bible heroes, one has to read many chapters and sometimes an entire book of the Bible. Since each of these sessions was designed to fit a class period of approximately an hour, there is not time for that type of study, nor is it age appropriate. Therefore, these heroes' stories are given in a synopsis instead of reading specific Scripture passages. Interactive stories, plays, and group projects are used to communicate information about Bible heroes.

Course Overview

Unit Aim:

Students learn that Bible heroes have a personal faith in God that compels them to follow, obey, and serve Him, regardless of the circumstances.

Session 1: Heroes Have Faith in God

Students learn that God used Bible heroes of the Pentateuch because they had faith in Him. Students learn how to have faith in God and in His promises. This session is presented through a "talk show" sketch that interviews specific Bible heroes.

Session 2: Heroes Obey God

Using heroes from the time of the Judges and Kings, students learn that when the Israelite heroes obeyed God, their nation prospered and was kept safe. When they disobeyed, sin reigned and the Israelites suffered. Students learn that our obedience to God affects both ourselves and others. Students create illustrations of a Bible hero.

Session 3: Heroes Are Faithful Through Trials

Using heroes from the prophetic period, students learn there may be special trials in this world as a result of their commitment to God. Students explore how to cope with temptations and problems that they might face as a result of their faith in Christ. Students participate in interactive Bible stories to learn about heroes.

Session 4: Heroes Tell Others About Jesus

Students understand that New Testament heroes shared their faith in Christ, even when that faith risked their lives. Students present a play introducing New Testament characters. (This play is included in the **Bridge the Gap** session. Students will present the play for their parents.) In closing, students identify people who are witnesses for Christ in today's world.

Bridge the Gap

This session provides an opportunity for parent and child interaction and for parents to hear the message of Jesus Christ. Students will present the play from Session 4. Two parents, selected in advance, share their testimony. A minister or lay leader gives an invitation to accept Christ. Read through this session at the beginning of this unit as it requires advance preparation in scheduling these special presentations.

Go to Extremes

Continuing with the theme of Session 4, students learn to communicate their personal faith in Christ. Students review what it means to be a Christian and explore how to share the message with others.

Teaching Tips

You may find the following information helpful in teaching this unit:

1. Read the session in advance so additional supplies can be gathered and preparations can be made.

2. Encourage students to bring Bibles, or have Bibles available for students' use.

3. Team teaching is recommended so that each small group will have a discussion leader. If a second teacher or youth assistant is not available, do not divide into small groups. This age group does not discuss well without an adult leading the discussion.

4. Be sensitive to students who may have no prior knowledge of the Bible. Your class may be at different levels of Bible understanding. As you play games and review, look for ways to encourage students in their Bible learning. Avoid embarrassing them for not knowing an answer.

5. Because this unit contains so much information regarding Bible heroes, emphasis was placed on heroes and the basic concepts that tie them together (i.e., obedience, faith). Memorization of a weekly theme verse is optional.

Personal Reflection

Studying these great men and women of faith is an inspiration and encouragement to our own faith. As we read and reread their stories, we see how much they are like us. We can glean insight into struggles we have as we see them struggle with sin, temptation, and difficulties. Like us, they were not perfect. God used them because they made themselves available. Take time this month to study some of these heroes from the

Scriptures. Below are some suggested characters and Scriptures. A Study Bible with notes would be helpful *(NIV Study Bible, NIV Student Bible, Life Application Bible).*

Eve	Genesis 2:19–4:26
Abraham and Sarah	Genesis 12–22
Joseph	Genesis 37–45
Ruth	Book of Ruth
Samson	Judges 13–16
Hannah	1 Samuel 1
Isaiah	Isaiah 6:1-13
Daniel	Daniel 1–6
John the Baptist	Luke 1, 3
Mary Magdalene	Luke 8:1-3; John 19:16–20:18
Paul	Acts 9:1-31
Stephen	Acts 6:1–7:60

The "Digging a Little Deeper" verse study (reproducible page 80) is designed for students to use every day. Verses relate to each session's theme. This helps students understand the theme and practice using their Bibles. It also helps to develop the habit of daily Bible reading. Prizes could be awarded to students who complete the project.

Digging a Little Deeper . . .

Read a verse every day.
Check (✓) the Scripture reference after you have read the verse.

• •

Week #1: We have faith in God.

❑ Deuteronomy 7:9

❑ Psalm 119:160

❑ Hebrews 11:1

❑ Hebrews 11:6

❑ Ephesians 2:8

❑ Galatians 3:26

❑ 2 Corinthians 5:7

❑ Mark 11:22, 23

Week #2: We obey God.

❑ Deuteronomy 11:26-28

❑ Philippians 4:9

❑ Matthew 7:24, 25

❑ Job 36:11

❑ John 15:10

❑ 1 John 2:17

❑ Psalm 106:3

❑ Romans 2:13

Week #3: We are faithful through trials.

❑ James 1:12

❑ Romans 12:12

❑ Romans 5:5

❑ Psalm 30:5

❑ Psalm 34:18

❑ Romans 8:31

❑ John 16:33

Week #4: We share Jesus with others.

❑ Acts 1:8

❑ 1 Peter 3:15

❑ Acts 4:20

❑ Matthew 10:19, 20

❑ 2 Timothy 4:2

❑ Ephesians 6:19

❑ Matthew 28:19, 20

Session 1

Heroes Have Faith in God

Scripture. Hebrews 11:1

Aim. Students learn that God used these Bible heroes because they had faith in Him.

Heroes. Adam, Eve, Abel, Noah, Abraham, Sarah, Isaac, Jacob, Joseph, Miriam, Moses, Rahab, Joshua

Get Into the Game

As students arrive, give them each a sheet of paper. Instruct them to illustrate a Bible hero or Bible story that is meaningful to them. (If some in the group are not familiar with Bible characters, help them choose an appropriate hero to illustrate from history.) After about five minutes, break up into two groups. Have students show and explain their drawings. Close the activity with this prayer: "Dear God, thank You for the many lessons You teach us through the heroes of the Bible. Help us listen and learn how these heroes' stories can help us in our walk with You. Amen."

Materials

paper, markers, crayons, or colored pencils

Step 1

Begin by telling the students, "We will be learning about Bible heroes and how they fit into Bible history. We will explore what made them heroes and how God used them to accomplish great things. All these heroes had one thing in common." Have the students look up and read Hebrews 11:1, 6, then ask the following questions:

1. According to these verses, what must we have to please God? (faith)

2. What are some key words that describe faith? (sure, certain, believe)

Say to the students, "How do we know that when we walk out of this room there will be air to breathe? Can we see it? Can we touch it? How do we know that it is there? We trust. We have faith it is there, and we don't worry whether or not we will be able to breathe. This is how our heroes felt about God and His promises. They believed even though they could not always see and touch what they were promised. God used the heroes we will study today because of their faith in Him."

Activity #1—
Lifestyles of the Righteous and Faithful

To introduce today's Bible heroes, students will participate in a "talk show." Distribute a photocopy of pages 84, 85 to each cast member. Set up the room with eight chairs in front and a microphone for a prop. Each character sits in a chair facing the rest of the class, who make up the studio audience.

Materials
photocopies of pages 84, 85

Activity #2—Hero Review

Divide students into two teams, one X and the other O. Draw a tic-tac-toe grid on a sheet of newsprint or a chalkboard. Using the statements that follow, begin with team X and ask them to name the hero being described. If the answer is correct, they chose where to put their X. If they are incorrect, the other team has a chance to guess. If neither answer correctly, move on to another question. Continue until one team gets three of their symbols in a row or until all the spaces are filled, making it a "tie." (Note: The team should work together to agree on an answer instead of relying on individual answers. To make this activity easier, put the names of all the characters on a sheet of newsprint or on the chalkboard so the students can choose from the heroes listed. This is recommended if you have a large group of students unfamiliar with the Bible.)

Materials
markers and newsprint or chalk and chalkboard

Tic-Tac-Toe Statements

1. His sacrifice was pleasing to God. (Abel)
2. God used him to save his family from a famine. (Joseph)
3. God used him to take his people out of slavery. (Moses)
4. She laughed when God promised her a son. (Sarah)
5. She hid her baby brother in a basket. (Miriam)
6. He used tricks to get his brother's blessing and birthright. (Jacob)
7. He was the promised child of Abraham. (Isaac)
8. She was saved because she helped spies. (Rahab)
9. She was the first mother. (Eve)
10. He was promised a nation would come from his children. (Abraham)
11. He was sent out of a garden for not obeying God. (Adam)
12. He trusted God and built a boat even though it had never rained. (Noah)
13. He miraculously took the city of Jericho by marching around its walls for six days. (Joshua)

Step 2

Divide students into two groups and work through "Gotta Have Faith." Through small group discussion, students will look at

Materials
photocopies of page 86

the lessons learned from Bible heroes and apply Bible promises to real life situations.

Say, "The Bible tells us that faith is being certain of what God has promised (Hebrews 11:1). We can have faith in what God has promised, just like our Bible heroes did."

Step 3

Students will begin making a time line using all the heroes listed below. Divide students into four groups. Each group works on three to four heroes using one "Time Line" page for each hero. The heroes are: Adam, Eve, Abel, Noah, Abraham, Sarah, Isaac, Jacob, Miriam, Moses, Joshua, Rahab. (Not all of these heroes were part of the "cast" in the talk show; however, information was communicated through the sketch.) Beginning with Adam, hang the time line on the wall so that students can see the chronological order and review the characters.

Materials
photocopies of page 87

Take It to the Next Level

Before students leave, distribute copies of "Family Feedback." The students will take these home and interview their parents about their favorite heroes, past and present. Remind the students to bring the sheets to next week's session so they can present them before the class. Close the session with the following prayer: "Dear God, thank You for the many wonderful examples of faith You have given us through these Bible heroes. Help us to look to Your promises and have faith in them. In Jesus' name, amen."

Materials
photocopies of page 88

Lifestyles of the Righteous and Faithful

Cast:
Reuben Leviticus (host)
Noah
Rahab
Joseph

Abel
Sarah
Jacob
Miriam

Reuben: Good evening. This is your host, Reuben Leviticus. Today's show includes those heroes who were present at the beginning of the world. These heroes followed God to prepare a people, the Israelites, among whom Jesus would be born many years later. Our first hero is Abel. Abel, did I hear you have famous parents?

Abel: My parents, Adam and Eve, were the first parents . . . actually, the first people. They were able to live in a beautiful paradise and have everything until . . .

Reuben: Until what? Why would anyone want to leave paradise?

Abel: Well, they didn't want to leave, but they had to because of a choice they made. They chose to disobey God, which was sin. God asked them not to eat from a special tree, and they chose to do it anyway. God was very sad. Because of their sin, they had to leave paradise. I tried to please God with my sacrifices. I knew that God required my first and best livestock as an offering for my sin. I offered my best because I loved God and wanted to show my appreciation for Him. My brother Cain did not understand. Cain gave God his leftovers. He became jealous when God blessed my sacrifices, so Cain murdered me.

Reuben: Thank you, Abel. Noah, what was it like to love God when no one else did?

Noah: Difficult! We obeyed and pleased God, but our neighbors thought we were crazy. I told them that God was unhappy with their lifestyles, but they only laughed. God told me to build a big boat called an ark. This project took over 100 years. When it began to rain, my family and many animals were saved, but because everyone else refused to believe and repent, they were not saved.

Reuben: Well Noah, your faith not only makes you a hero, it saved your life. Let's hear from a hero who kept the faith even when it looked hopeless—Abraham's wife Sarah.

Sarah: God promised my husband would be the father of a new nation called the Israelites. When I was 90 years old, God promised me a son. I laughed because this seemed impossible. God forgave my laughter, and I had a son named Isaac, which means "he laughs." I laugh with joy because God can do the impossible when we have faith.

Reuben: Well, Abraham did become the father of a great nation, the Israelites. It was named Israel after one of your grandchildren, who was first called Jacob. Jacob, tell us about your faith in God.

Jacob: Even though my father was Isaac and my grandfather was Abraham, I learned about trusting God the hard way. I tried to take situations into my own hands. I stole the "birthright" and "blessing" from my brother, Esau. God promised my mother, Rebekah, I would be blessed, so I tried to make that happen without God. Because of this, I had to run for my life or be killed. God forgave me, and I learned from my mistake and trusted God for my faith and the faith of my family. Later God gave me the new name of Israel meaning "he who struggles with God," because I struggled to keep my faith and be obedient to Him.

Reuben: Great. Let's meet your son, Joseph, who saved you, your children, and your grandchildren because of his great faith.

Joseph: I don't know if my faith was always great, but I tried to be faithful to God. Even when my brothers mistreated me, sold me into slavery, and my master unfairly accused me of a crime, I kept my faith in God. I knew God had a plan for me. Because I helped people in prison, I was recommended to help the Pharaoh. I became second in command of Egypt. God used my position to give my father, my brothers, and their families food during a famine.

Reuben: Thank you, Joseph. Next we have a sister who risked everything to save her brother.

Miriam: Four hundred years later, the Israelites were still in Egypt. But Pharaoh felt threatened because there were so many Israelites, so he made them his slaves. When he ordered that all baby boys be killed, we didn't kill my brother, Moses. I hid him in a basket in the water where he was discovered by a princess and raised in the Pharaoh's palace. My mother was hired as his nurse to care for him. She told him about our Israelite history and never let him forget who he was. Moses grew up to lead our people out of Egypt and out of slavery. Through Moses, God gave His people the Ten Commandments, which showed us how God wants us to live. Because of Moses' faith, God used him to accomplish great things.

Reuben: Thank you, Miriam. Rahab, you are listed in the book of Hebrews as a great woman of faith. Tell me your story.

Rahab: I was not an Israelite; I was a citizen of Jericho. Joshua (Israel's leader after Moses died) captured our city after marching around it for six days. On the seventh day, they blew horns and the walls of the city crashed down. But before this capture, Joshua sent spies to Jericho. After I met them, I knew that their God was the one true God. I hid the spies from the King of Jericho, risking my life. Because of my courage, when Joshua captured Jericho, my life was spared.

Reuben: Thank you, Rahab, for your story of faith. Well, that's our show for today. I hope you, our studio audience, can find some lessons of faith from these heroes.

Bible Promise

"Give, and it will be given to you. A good measure, pressed down, shaken together and running over, will be poured into your lap. For with measure you use, it will be measured to you." (Luke 6:38)

Abel gave his first and best to God. How can you give your first and best to God? How can this verse help you have faith to give your best?

_____ Give first 10 percent of allowance/earnings as offering.

_____ Use abilities God has given me to serve Him at church.

_____ Give time to help others on a regular basis.

_____ Spend time with God by praying and reading the Bible.

- - - - - - - - - - -

Bible Promise

"This is the assurance we have in approaching God: that if we ask anything according to his will, he hears us. And if we know that he hears us—whatever we ask—we know that we have what we asked of him." (1 John 5:14, 15)

Abraham had faith in God even when he could not see the answer to his prayer. Name something you have prayed for. Has God answered yet? How could faith in the Bible promise help you with prayer?

- - - - - - - - - - -

Bible Promise

"I can do everything through him who gives me strength." (Philippians 4:13)

At first, Moses did not want to lead the people out of slavery. He was afraid and did not feel confident that he could do it. How you would respond in these situations? How can this Bible promise help you?

1. All the kids make fun of Kevin. He stutters when he speaks. As he answers a question in class, all the kids around you are laughing and trying to get you to laugh at him. What would God want you to do?

2. You feel that God wants you to invite Greg to Vacation Bible School. You resist because you are afraid Greg might make fun of your faith. What would you do?

— Time Line —

Copy this sheet for every hero that will be used in the time line as described in each session. Working in groups, students will prepare one sheet for each Bible hero. (Note: Teacher may have to review and give suggestions for story or symbols. Remember, this sheet will be used in all four sessions!)

_____
(Bible Hero)

Write a sentence describing hero: _____

_____

_____

(Draw a story or symbol of the hero.)

Family Feedback

Take this paper home and interview your parent(s).

1. When you were ten or eleven years old, who was your hero? Why?

2. Name a person who would be a hero now. Why?

Dear Parent: For the next four sessions, your preteen will be exploring the lives and lessons of major Bible heroes. If you feel comfortable, talk about Bible characters that have been an inspiration to you as you think of heroes for the above questions. This would also be a good time to review Bible stories during a family time. A Bible story book would be a good resource for this. There are many available at your local Christian bookstore.

Heroes Obey God

Scripture. Deuteronomy 11:26-28

Aim. Students learn that when Israelite heroes obey God, their nation prospers and is kept safe. When they disobey, sin reigns and the Israelites suffer.

Heroes. Deborah, Gideon, Samson, Ruth, Hannah, Samuel, Saul, David, Solomon

Get Into the Game

Write the alphabet on a chalkboard or on newsprint. Using their Bibles for help, students take turns writing a Bible character that begins with a letter listed on the chalkboard. Students should cross out the letter after it has been used. Close the activity with this prayer: "Dear God, thank You that we can learn from Your Bible heroes. Prepare our hearts to learn how we also can be used by You. In Jesus' name, amen."

Materials

chalk and chalkboard or markers and newsprint

Step 1

Ask the students to open their Bibles to the book of Judges, then say, "The book of Judges is about heroes God used to lead the Israelites. A judge was a leader of the Israelite people who provided both spiritual and military leadership. We will also be studying kings who ruled Israel." (Direct students to the table of contents in their Bibles.) "These heroes were recorded in 1 and 2 Samuel, 1 and 2 Kings, and 1 and 2 Chronicles. During this time period, the Israelite nation floundered from obedience to disobedience." Have students look up Deuteronomy 11:26-28 and read it aloud. Ask students the following questions:

1. What does God promise if the people obey? (a blessing)
2. What will happen if they disobey? (a curse)

Tell the students, "When the people obeyed and worshiped God, their nation enjoyed peace and prosperity. They were able to overcome other nations who tried to rule them. However, as time went on, the Israelites would get curious about worshiping other gods from surrounding nations. They would get careless about God's laws. They would stop taking care of each other and neglect the poor. Worst of all, they would stop worshiping the Lord their God. When this happened, the nation of Israel suffered. Other nations would take

Materials

white 8½-by-11-inch paper, thin markers or colored pencils, photocopies of pages 91-93

them captive creating much suffering. God used heroes we call Judges and Kings to help call the people back to Him. These heroes were not perfect—but they obeyed and were used by God."

Divide the class into pairs. Give each pair a sheet of paper and thin markers or colored pencils. From reproducible pages 91-93, assign each pair one or two heroes to study. Be sure to assign all of the heroes. (If you have fewer than ten students, groups may have two or three heroes to study.) Students should read the character study and make up a cartoon or illustrated story to present to the class describing how the hero obeyed or disobeyed God. Allow fifteen minutes for them to prepare their assignments. When everyone has finished, have the students present their drawings to the class. (Note: Students work from information given in the paragraphs, not in the listed Scripture passage. Scripture references are given to help students understand where these characters are found in the Bible. Most Scripture passages are too long for students to read in this time frame.)

Step 2

When all groups have finished their presentations, have students return to their original pairs. Distribute the "Time Line" pages and have students complete them. When students have finished, hang the new time line contributions on the wall.

Materials
photocopies of page 87

Step 3

Divide the class into two groups. Discuss each situation on page 94 and decide how the choice affects themselves and others.

Materials
photocopies of page 94

Take It to the Next Level

Distribute "Family Feedback" (page 95) for students to take home. Working with a parent, students will choose from selected heroes to learn lessons of obedience from a hero's life. Challenge the students to bring the completed page to next week's session. Close the session with this prayer: "Dear Jesus, thank You for giving us rules to live by. We know that You give them to us to protect us from harm. Help us to obey and look to You for direction. In Jesus' name, amen."

Materials
photocopies of page 95

✤ Deborah ✣

(Judges 4:1-24)

Because the Israelite people had stopped obeying God, God allowed the Israelite people to be sold into the hands of wicked King Jabin. When the people cried for deliverance, God brought up a leader named Deborah. She ruled with wisdom and faithfulness to God. Deborah called her top military man, Barak, and asked for his leadership. He said he would fight, but only if she would go also. After they won the battle, Deborah gave the credit to God in the form of a song recorded in Judges 5:1-31. She taught the Israelite people to obey God, and she led them to repentance and faithfulness. Because of Deborah's faithfulness, there was peace in the land for forty years. From Deborah we can learn that when we are willing and faithful, God will use us for His purposes.

✦ Gideon ✦

(Judges 6–8)

The Israelites walked away from God and did evil in His sight. The Lord allowed them to be under the power of the evil Midianites. The Midianites stole the Israelite's crops and livestock leaving them poor and hungry. Many Israelites lived in caves to hide from the Midianites. When the people finally cried out to God for help, God answered by calling Gideon to deliver them. Gideon was reluctant at first because he felt insecure in his abilities to do the job and because his family was very poor. The first thing God asked him to do was destroy an idol that the Israelites had put up for the worship of Baal. (Baal was a false god that the Midianites worshiped.) Asking Gideon to take down this altar was the first step in helping the people get back to God. Then God asked Gideon to defeat 15,000 Midianites in battle. To do this, God asked a strange thing of Gideon. He told him to reduce the Israelite army from 32,000 to 300! How could he win with only 300 men? God did this to show the Israelites that this battle would be won because of God's presence, not by the strength of man. The Midianites were defeated. Because of Gideon's obedience, the nation of Israel was saved. While Gideon ruled, he taught the people to repent and obey God. From Gideon we learn that even though we feel we have little to offer God, He can take the little we have and multiply it.

✣ Samson ✣

(Judges 13–16)

The Israelites did evil in the sight of God, so they were captured by the Philistines. The people cried out for deliverance. In time Samson was born into a God-fearing Israelite family. His parents knew that this son would be special because his birth was predicted by an angel. The angel gave them specific instructions to raise him to be a leader for God. Samson had unusual physical strength that was attributed to the "spirit of God." With this strength, he was successful in fighting the Philistines. But Samson became judge to the Israelites. But Samson became proud and boasted of his strength. He began to use it for selfish reasons and for revenge. Several times he got into trouble because he was not careful in his relationships. Because of his strong love for Delilah, Samson revealed the secret of his strength—his long hair. Delilah immediately cut his hair, and Samson became weak. He was taken prisoner by the Philistines. Samson had obeyed God and rescued the Israelites from the Philistines, but he ended up using the gifts for his own selfish purposes. This eventually led to his own destruction. From Samson we learn not to waste the gifts God gave us. We should not use our gifts for selfish purposes. We want to keep following God.

✝ Ruth ✝
(Book of Ruth)

The book of Ruth tells us about a godly woman who was not born an Israelite. Ruth, a Moabitess, married an Israelite. Through this marriage, she came to know the one true God. Famine and tragedy hit her household leaving her husband, husband's brother, and father-in-law dead. Naomi, Ruth's mother-in-law, decided to return to her homeland, Bethlehem. She told Ruth and Ruth's sister-in-law Orpah to return to their families so that they could have a better life. Orpah did return home. But Ruth was committed to stay with Naomi. She wanted to take care of her and remain part of the family that helped her find the true God. Naomi and Ruth returned to Bethlehem. In Bethlehem, Ruth took care of Naomi by working in the fields and picking up grain left by the harvesters. The owner of the field, Boaz, was impressed by Ruth's care for Naomi. When he discovered she was a widow, he married her. Ruth and Boaz had a son who became the grandfather of King David. Ruth teaches us that as we are obedient to our responsibilities, and put God and others first, God will take care of us and our future.

✿ Hannah ✿
(1 Samuel 1:1-28)

Hannah was sad because she was unable to have children. One day, Hannah went to the synagogue to pray for a child. She promised God that if she could have a son she would give him back to God. God answered her prayer and within a year, Hannah gave birth to a son, Samuel. When Samuel was about four years old, Hannah took him to the temple and dedicated him to God's service. Hannah had to leave Samuel at the temple to be raised by the priest. This was a very difficult promise to keep because Hannah had waited so long for this child. He was very precious to her. After Hannah gave Samuel to God, God gave her five more children. From Hannah we learn that God listens to our prayers and honors our promise-keeping.

❖ Samuel ❖
(1 Samuel 3:1-21)

Samuel was a very special child. He had a special relationship with God. When he was very young, Samuel was dedicated to God and taken to the temple to be raised by the priest. He grew up under the direction of Eli, the priest. Samuel assisted Eli in the temple. When Samuel was still a child, God spoke to him in the middle of the night, telling him things that would be happening and giving him instructions about what he was to do. Samuel listened and obeyed God. Samuel was a willing servant and continued to grow in his faith, wisdom, and obedience to God. As an adult, Samuel was used by God to anoint the first two kings of Israel, Saul and David. He served as their trusted advisor and prophet.

Samuel teaches us that God will use us even while we are children if we are faithful, obedient, and willing to serve.

✦ Solomon ✦

(2 Samuel–1 Kings 11:43)

Solomon was King David's son and chosen heir to the throne. Solomon had many advantages helping him learn to be king. He had a godly example in his father, a strong education and much wealth. Solomon began his reign with godliness. God granted Solomon's wish for wisdom to rule his people. During Solomon's early reign he directed the building of the temple to help the people worship God. Solomon led Israel in faithful obedience to God, and Israel prospered. Then Solomon began to get distracted. He started accumulating wives from other nations, and they began to worship other gods. Solomon also started relying on himself instead of God. He stopped ruling the people with compassion and wisdom and began abusing them through heavy taxation and slave labor. Unfortunately, Solomon never repented. Because of his poor leadership, the Kingdom became divided after his death. Solomon teaches us that even if we have the advantage of wealth and wisdom, we cannot use it well unless we put God first.

❖ David ❖

(1 Samuel 16–1 Kings 2)

Although David was an adult when he became the second king of Israel, God was preparing him from childhood. When David was young, he worked as a shepherd. He learned responsibility for the sheep and did his job with excellence. He gained courage and boldness through protecting the sheep from prowling lions and wolves. David respected his father and obeyed when he was asked to take some food to his brothers who were fighting the Philistines. David found his brothers and the Israelite army trembling in fear of the giant, Goliath. Because David knew the power of God, he did not understand why the Israelites were afraid. When David volunteered to confront Goliath, the people laughed at him because he was young and not a trained soldier. But David was brave; with confidence he called on God to help him save the Israelites. Using a slingshot and a few smooth stones, David defeated Goliath. David became king of Israel following Saul's death. David was not perfect; he sinned and the nation of Israel suffered. But most of the time, David sought to obey and follow God. Because of his faithfulness, he is known as the greatest king of Israel. We can learn from David that God is preparing and working in us even when we are young.

✢ Saul ✢

(1 Samuel 9–31)

Saul was the first king of the Israelite nation. Before Saul, the Israelites looked to God as their "king" and had an earthly "judge" or mediator as their leader. Because other nations had kings, the Israelites demanded to be ruled by a king. They wanted to be like the other nations. God knew having an earthly human ruler would bring problems, but he let the people have their way. Saul was a handsome and strong leader. When he humbled himself and obeyed God, he was a powerful leader and the Israelites prospered. But Saul became proud and conceited. He began to take decisions into his own hands. Because he was unfaithful, God raised another leader, David. Saul became so jealous of David, he tried to kill him. Saul's life ended tragically as he destroyed himself with his bitterness and prideful spirit. The lesson of Saul shows us that even if we have many talents and advantages, we need to live in obedience to God to truly be happy and fulfill our potential.

Choices...

1 You are selected in gym class to choose teams for softball. You know one girl never gets picked until last. Will you pick her or will you pick the ones whom you know are good players? How will your decision affect others?

2 You are a valuable member of your church's choir. There is a special program coming up, and you have been asked to sing a solo. You have also been invited to a party at a friend's house for the same night and time. Which will you choose? How does your decision affect others?

3 You are horsing around with your football in the living room and break a lamp. You know that if you blame it on your preschool brother, your mom would probably believe you. What will you choose to tell her? How will your decision affect others?

4 You are studying evolution in science class. A friend from church asks you what you think about evolution versus creation. Lots of kids are standing around listening. Do you answer by sharing your faith in God? How will your decision affect others?

5 You are spending the night at a friend's house. A TV show comes on that your parents do not let you watch because of the violent content. However, they would probably never know that you watched it. Do you watch it? How would your decision affect others?

Family Feedback

Choose one hero and look up the Scripture reference to discover how God used that person. Work with a parent to answer the questions.

Heroes
Abigail (AB-eh-gale)   1 Samuel 25:1-35
Josiah (jo-SY-uh)   2 Kings 22:1-13; 23:1-3
Asa (AY-sah)   2 Chronicles 14:2-7; 15:1-15

Name of hero:_____

1. Did the hero obey God? If yes, how?

2. What happened as a result of the person's obedience?

3. Do you think this person was a hero? Why or why not?

Attention parent: This week we studied how our obedience to God affects ourselves and others. As you are working through this sheet, look for examples of how the hero was affected by his or her choices and how these choices impacted those around them.

Heroes Are Faithful Through Trials

Scripture. James 1:12

Aim. Students learn there may be special trials in this world as a result of their commitment to God, but God is faithful. He will help them persevere.

Heroes. Elijah, Jonah, Isaiah, Daniel, Esther, Nehemiah

Get Into the Game

Using characters studied in the previous sessions, write the names of the Bible heroes on small index cards. Tape the cards onto the backs of students as they arrive. Have students discover their characters' names by asking *yes* or *no* questions. (If you have visitors who may be unfamiliar with the Bible, include a few famous people such as Abraham Lincoln or Martin Luther King.)

After five minutes, close with this prayer, "Dear God, thank You for always being with us, even through difficult times. Help us learn from our Bible heroes so we can face temptations and trials while remaining faithful to You. In Jesus' name, amen."

Materials
index cards, masking tape

Step 1

Say to the students, "Today we are going to learn about some heroes that endured difficult and risky situations, but remained faithful to God. We will study a queen and a prince who took big risks. The other heroes were prophets. Prophets were special messengers sent by God to call the people back to obedience to God. Prophets warned the people of disaster if they did not follow God. Many times the people made fun of the prophets, or even worse, killed them. Both Esther and the prophets knew it was worth the risk to follow God because their reward was not on this earth." Have students find James 1:12 and read it aloud. "This verse reminds us that following God may not always be easy, but God will reward our faithfulness."

Begin by using pages 98–103. Read through the interactive stories and have the students participate as directed. Students

Materials
photocopies of pages 98–103

are directed by the teacher, who narrates from the story sheet. The key to making interactive stories effective is to "ham it up."

Divide students into three groups and assign one story per group. Give students five minutes to create their own interactive story using either format given or creating their own. Have them present their stories to the class.

Step 2

Divide students into groups of two or three to complete time line pages for the six heroes. Give students the appropriate copy of an interactive Bible story (pages 98–103) as a guide. Display time line contributions on the wall when completed.

Materials
photocopies of pages 87, 98–103

Step 3

Divide the class into two groups and discuss "Sticky Situations." There are no right or wrong answers for these situations. Students are to think of how to live out their Christian faith in the face of potential risks.

Materials
photocopies of page 104

Take It to the Next Level

Challenge students to take home "Family Feedback" (page 105) and interview a parent. Close the session with this prayer: "Dear God, help us to remember that You are with us this week. Help us to always be faithful, seeking strength from You when we need help or direction. In Jesus' name, amen."

Materials
photocopies of page 105

Esther

Read the story. As character's names are read, students make sound effects as directed in the box below. (Names are highlighted in boldface type for your aid.)

Esther *("wolf whistle")*
Mordecai *(clap and yell, "Yeah!")*
Xerxes *(stand up at attention and yell, "Long live the king!")*
Haman *(yell, "Boo!")*

Once upon a time their was a young Jewish girl named **Esther. Esther's** parents died, but she was adopted by a loving cousin, **Mordecai. Mordecai** worked in the palace for **King Xerxes. Esther** grew to be a beautiful and intelligent woman. When **King Xerxes** was looking for a queen, **Mordecai** brought **Esther** for his approval. **King Xerxes** was impressed with her and made **Esther** queen of all his kingdom. **Mordecai** continued to work in the palace and also helped as **Esther's** advisor. There was a wicked man named **Haman** who was second in command to **King Xerxes. Mordecai** would not bow down and worship **Haman,** so **Haman** decided to plot against him. Knowing that **Mordecai** was Jewish, **Haman** made a decree that all Jews would be killed. **Mordecai** approached **Esther** and asked for her help to get this decree overruled by **King Xerxes. Mordecai** told **Esther** that God had allowed her to become queen at this time to save her people. **Esther** knew her life was at risk if she went into the presence of **King Xerxes** without being invited, but she did. **Esther** asked **King Xerxes** to a banquet. **King Xerxes** asked what **Esther** wanted, but instead of telling him, she invited him to another banquet the next day. At the second banquet given by **Queen Esther, King Xerxes, Mordecai,** and **Haman** were sitting at the head table. **King Xerxes** asked **Esther** what she desired. She revealed the plot to kill the Jews and announced that **Haman** was the culprit. **King Xerxes** executed **Haman.** The Jewish people were saved because of **Esther** and **Mordecai's** bravery. From **Esther** we learn that God will strengthen us and help us be brave as we seek to do His work.

The Prophet

Jonah

Select students for characters as directed below. Characters should follow the directions given in parentheses. One or more students can lead others to participate where audience participation is requested.

Jonah *(audience applauds when name is mentioned)*
God *(voice only)*
Boat *(2 kids holding hands standing face to face about 2-3 feet apart so Jonah can stand in middle)*
Great Fish *(student stands with hands straight out and claps them together like a fish with big mouth)*

Once upon a time there was a prophet named **Jonah**. *(Everyone applauds for Jonah.)* God told **Jonah** to go and preach to the people in Nineveh. *(Student playing God says, "Go to Nineveh," in a deep voice.)* **Jonah** was scared. *(Jonah makes a scared expression.)* **Jonah** hated the Ninevites because they were a wicked people. *(Audience yells, "Boo Nineveh!")* **Jonah** was afraid they would hurt him, so he ran away. *(Jonah runs in place for 15 seconds while audience counts to 15.)* **Jonah** jumped on a boat. *(Jonah jumps into the boat.)* The boat began to rock and sway with a mighty storm. *(Boat rocks and rocks throwing Jonah around. Have audience make thunder, wind, and splash sound effects.)* Finally, **Jonah** is thrown off the boat. *(Boat picks Jonah up and throws him.)* **Jonah** is swallowed by a fish. *(Student playing fish grabs him. Jonah holds nose and says, "Phew!")* Finally, **Jonah** confesses his disobedience to God and agrees to go to Nineveh. *(Jonah gets on knees with folded hands and looks up to God.)* After three days, the fish threw **Jonah** up. *(Fish looks and acts like he is vomiting.)* **Jonah** ran to Nineveh. *(Run in place for 15 seconds. Have audience count.)* He preached to the people. *(Have Jonah yell, "Repent! Repent! Repent!")* The people repented, changed their ways and believed in God. The people were saved because **Jonah** finally obeyed God. **Jonah** teaches us not to be afraid when God calls us to take a risk.

The Prophet
Elijah

Select students for characters as directed below. Characters follow the directions given in parentheses. Have all students participate where indicated with boldface type.

Elijah
Jezebel
Ahab
2-3 Baal prophets
2 altars *(4 students paired up, arms outstretched making a circle)*
Fire *(student hiding in God's altar)*
Audience participation *(When teacher reads these words, audience responds as follows)*
    Elijah: *(audience puts hands on heart)*
    One true God: *"He's number one!"*
    Baal: *"Boo!"*

Elijah was faithful to the **one true God** and served Him valiantly. *(Elijah puts hand on his heart.)* **Elijah** was called by God to confront the wicked King Ahab *(evil laugh)* and his wife Jezebel *(evil laugh).* **Elijah** challenged King Ahab to a contest to prove his God was the **one true God** instead of the false god **Baal** worshiped by the King and Queen. **Elijah** built two altars. *(Students playing altars go up. Elijah pretends to hammer and build them. Fire hides in God's altar.)* **Elijah** built one for **Baal,** and one for the **one true God.** Only the **one true god** would bring fire and light to the altar. King Ahab, Queen Jezebel, and the **Baal** prophets danced around their altar until they were exhausted. *(King, Queen, and prophets dance around the altar then collapse in front it.)* They begged and pleaded. *(Plead on their knees.)* But nothing happened. Then it was **Elijah's** turn. **Elijah** knelt down and prayed to the **one true God.** *(Elijah kneels and folds hand to pray.)* God sent fire to consume the altar. *(Fire jumps up from inside altar and says, "Whoosh.")* **Elijah** proved his God to be the **one true God.** Because of **Elijah's** bravery, many people turned away from **Baal** and believed in the **one true God.**

The Prophet

Daniel

Make a happy face and a sad face out of yellow construction paper. As the narrator reads, everyone else in group holds up a happy or sad face. Have audience yell "Yeah!" when the group holds up a happy face and "Boo!" when they hold up a sad face. (A ☺ equals a happy face; an ☹ equals a sad face.)

King Nebuchadnezzar ☹, the ruler of Babylon, was looking for some of the captive Israelites to serve him in the palace. Daniel was one of those chosen because of his exceptional intelligence, character, and good looks ☺. When in the palace, Daniel refused to eat the diet provided by the King because it was high in fat and rich foods. ☹ It also included foods that Jews were forbidden to eat. ☹ Daniel negotiated with the King to continue his diet of fruits and vegetables and be tested at the end of the month to see if he was as healthy as his peers who were eating the King's diet. At the end of the month, Daniel was healthier than the rest of the men. ☺ During King Darius' rule, Daniel became so powerful ☺ that some of the other palace staff became jealous. ☹ Knowing that Daniel faithfully worshiped God ☺, they plotted to make a rule that would make worship of anyone but the king unlawful. ☹ Daniel continued praying and worshipping God. ☺ The other men caught him and brought him before King Darius to face charges. Daniel was thrown into the den of lions. ☹ The Lord shut the mouths of the lions. ☺ He was saved! ☺ The King made a new decree: "Everyone must worship the one true God." ☺ Daniel teaches us to stay true to our convictions even in the face of danger. ☺

The Prophet

Isaiah

Select students for characters as directed below. Characters follow the directions given in parentheses.

Narrator *(reads story)*
Isaiah
Angels *(2-4 students)*
Throne *(2 students kneeling to make throne)*
God *(sits on 2 students making throne)*

Isaiah is a great prophet. The Lord spoke to him through visions. *(Isaiah puts hand on forehead as if looking for something in the distance.)* Isaiah saw God sitting on a throne. *(Throne and "God" take places.)* Around him there were angels. *(Angels surround throne.)* Because of God's holiness, the angels covered their eyes. *(Angels cover eyes.)* They covered their feet. *(Angels cover feet.)* The angels said, "Holy, Holy, Holy is the Lord God almighty." *(Angels repeat.)* Isaiah was filled with awe. *(Isaiah falls down to his knees.)* Isaiah heard God say, "Whom shall I send?" Isaiah answered, "Here I am, send me." *(Isaiah jumps up and repeats this to character playing God.)* As prophet, he called people to repent and obey God. God gave him messages to tell the Israelites, but also warned him that they would not be receptive. Isaiah would not be popular because the people would not want to turn from their wicked ways. Later in Isaiah's ministry, God gave him prophecies of the coming Messiah, which are recorded both in Isaiah and in the New Testament. Isaiah shows us that people who follow God and do the right things may still suffer. Heaven is one reward for those who are faithful to God.

Nehemiah

Select students for characters as directed below. Characters follow the directions given in parentheses.

Narrator *(reads story)*
Nehemiah
Workers *(rest of students in group)*
(use play blocks or Legos for props)
(Narrator stands in front of group building the wall. While narrator reads, Nehemiah is silently directing workers to build the walls of the city. Workers begin stacking play blocks to make a wall.)

Nehemiah was a cupbearer in the service of King Artaxerxes. *(Narrator introduces Nehemiah who then goes back to directing the building of the wall.)* Nehemiah prayed for his people, the Israelites. Their city, Jerusalem, had been in ruins for many years. Although a group of exiles had returned and rebuilt the temple ninety years earlier, the walls of the city still lay in ruin. City walls were very important because they offered safety from raids and symbolized peace and strength. Nehemiah believed God was calling him to Jerusalem to redirect the building of the walls. King Artaxerxes let Nehemiah go back to Jerusalem. The governor of a surrounding area hoped to rule the city of Jerusalem. *(Governor steps in front of wall and crosses his arms to symbolize anger.)* He tried to prevent the Jews from helping Nehemiah. *(Governor mimes yelling at workers.)* But Nehemiah prayed. *(Nehemiah gets on knees, prays, gets up, and resumes work. Governor exits stage.)* He refused to get discouraged and the work continued. Some men protected the workers. *(A few of the workers stand in front of walls with arms crossed having stern expressions on their faces.)* When the walls were almost completed, the governor was successful in turning some Israelites against him. But Nehemiah continued with determination and completed the building of the walls of Jerusalem. Nehemiah teaches us to obey and stay on track with the plans God gives us even if people make fun or don't agree with us.

Sticky Situations

1 Esther risked her important position and her life to obey God and save His people, the Israelites. Rebekah was sitting in the cafeteria when three of the popular girls started making fun of another girl who dressed funny. Should Rebekah:

a. Ask them to stop and say some nice things about the girl.

b. Ignore them and just not contribute to the conversation.

c. Join in and make jokes to be popular too.

d. Walk away from the group.

2 At first Jonah did not want to go to Nineveh and tell people about God. Mark's friend, Rich, doesn't believe in God. Should he:

a. Tell his church friends that Rich doesn't believe in God.

b. Invite Rich to a church activity.

c. Explain to Rich why he goes to church.

d. Say nothing so that Rich won't be offended.

3 Daniel was told he could not pray to God. Jared was told he could not pray in school. Should he:

a. Continue to pray quietly to himself.

b. Complain to other kids about the prayer rule.

c. Not do his schoolwork until they change the rule.

d. Stop praying at school and wait until he gets home.

Read James 1:12. What does God promise us as we go through difficult times?

FAMILY FEEDBACK

1 Ask your parent(s) to describe a time that was difficult (i.e., job change, college experience, childhood experience, death of a loved one).

2 How did it change their choices?

3 What helped them get through it? How did this help them?
   a. friends
   b. faith in God
   c. church
   d. family
   e. self
   f. Bible verse
   g. other _____

Dear parent: This week we studied Bible heroes whose faith was tested in difficult situations. Sometimes they even had to choose between their faith and their safety. We all face stressful situations and these Bible heroes learned how to effectively handle them with God's help. Share with your child an especially difficult time and how you got through it.

Session 4

Heroes Tell Others About Jesus

Scripture. Acts 1:8

Aim. Students will understand that the New Testament heroes lived and proclaimed their faith in Christ, even when those actions endangered their lives.

Heroes. John the Baptist, Nicodemus, Peter, Matthew, Mary Magdalene, Stephen, Paul, Priscilla

Get Into the Game

In advance, write the names of all the Bible heroes from the time line on small cards. Put cards in a paper bag. Divide students into two teams. One student takes a card and reads to his team. Working as a team, students give one sentence describing the character. If the team can describe or tell something about the hero, they get a point. If they cannot, the card goes back in the bag. The process repeats as the other team draws a card. Close the activity when cards are completed or when interest lags. Pray: "Dear God, thank You for the heroes who witnessed of their faith. Help us to learn and understand their message. In Jesus' name, amen."

Materials
index cards with hero's name written on each, paper bag

Step 1

Direct students to open their Bibles to the table of contents. Ask the following questions:

1. The Bible is divided into two parts. What are they?
2. Why is the Bible divided into two parts?

After students have a chance to offer their ideas, explain: "The Bible is divided into two parts, the Old Testament and the New Testament. The Old Testament tells of heroes who believed in God's promise of a Messiah. This Messiah would come and restore the Israelites' relationship with God. The New Testament tells of the fulfillment of that promise. God send Jesus, the Messiah. The New Testament tells us about Jesus and those heroes who gave witness to Him." Have students look up Acts 1:8 and have someone read it aloud. Then ask the following questions:

1. What did Jesus promise they would receive? (power, Holy Spirit)

Materials
photocopies of pages 109–112

2. What did Jesus command them to do? (be witnesses everywhere)

3. What is a witness? (someone who gives testimony of a person or an event)

Say to the students, "In our courts of law, we use witnesses to explain what they perceive happened in a specific circumstance. When you explain something you saw, you are giving witness to that event. Our New Testament heroes were considered witnesses because they gave witness, or shared, something they knew to be true. They shared their faith and belief in Jesus. Let's meet a few of these witnesses."

Using the script "Witnesses of Christ," select students for the characters listed. Present the play with students reading from the script. (Note: It is suggested that students also present this play for their parents during the **Bridge the Gap** bonus session.)

Step 2

Divide students into two groups. Using "Witnesses of Today," students will identify modern witnesses by circling persons they believe are witnesses for Christ. They should also write a few words describing how this person can be a witness. After they finish, explain that all of these persons could be witnesses. Give examples of how they could tell someone about Christ.

Materials
photocopies of page 113

Step 3

Have the students form pairs to complete the time line with the heroes from today's session. Use the scripts to help students with details. Hang the contributions on the time line wall. The play the following review game to help give students a chronological perspective of heroes.

Divide the students into two teams. Using the heroes listed below, ask one team to tell if the hero is from the New Testament or the Old Testament. Reward the team with a point if the answer is correct. If the answer is incorrect, do not use that hero name again. Play until all heroes' names have been called.

Materials
photocopies of page 87

Abraham	Daniel	Timothy
Joseph*	Mary Magdalene	Peter
John the Baptist	Noah	Saul
Gideon	Paul	Nicodemus
Aquila	Hannah	Stephen
Joshua	David	Jonah
Philip	Matthew	Esther

*There is a Joseph in both Testaments.

Take It to the Next Level

Students should take "Family Feedback" (page 114) home. This sheet will help students give information about themselves, which will help them explain their personal testimony of Christ. (See the **Go to Extremes** session.) Close the session with this prayer: "Dear Jesus, we praise Your name for these New Testament men and women who gave witness for You. Because of their testimony, we believe in You today. Please help us learn to tell people about Jesus as boldly as they did. In Jesus' name, amen."

Materials
photocopies of page 114

The People Challenge
Witnesses of Christ

Assign the following parts. Students may wait in audience until they are involved in the play. (Students not selected watch the play.) Prosecuting and defense attorneys should stand and face the judge when they speak.

Setting
(table in front of class with judge behind table; chair next to table for witness stand)

Props
(letter, Bible, small chain made out of paper strips, child's wooden hammer for a gavel)

Cast

Judge	**Caiaphas** *(Prosecuting Attorney)*
John the Baptist	**Nicodemus** *(Defense Attorney)*
Stephen	**Peter**
Mary Magdalene	**Matthew** *(holds Bible)*
Priscilla	**Paul** *(attach paper chain to his wrists)*

Judge: *(slam gavel)* We continue the trial of "The People Challenge Witnesses of Jesus Christ." This is a trial to decide if this new religion called Christianity is true. We will base our decision on an investigation of the man named Jesus Christ. Yesterday we heard from the prosecution. Today the defense will present their case. We will hear from several witnesses about their encounters with this man.

Nicodemus: I call John the Baptist to the stand. *(John the Baptist goes to witness stand.)*

Caiaphas: Your honor, I object to the way he is dressed. His camel-skin outfit is disrespectful for the courtroom. I move that he be found in contempt of court.

Nicodemus: Your honor, John is a prophet who lives in the desert. He has no need for fancy clothes, nor does he have the money to purchase them.

Judge: *(slam gavel)* Objection overruled.

Nicodemus: John, could you tell us who you believe Jesus to be?

John the Baptist: God called me to announce Jesus' coming. I was to prepare people by calling them to repentance. Jesus came to me and asked me to baptize Him. After I baptized Him, I heard God's voice say, "This is my Son in whom I am well pleased." I know Jesus is the true Son of God.

Nicodemus: Thank you. You may step down. I call the disciple Peter to the stand. *(John sits down and Peter steps up.)* Peter, tell us about your relationship with Jesus.

Peter: I was a fisherman until I met Jesus. I traveled with Jesus for three years. He changed my life and helped me change my weaknesses into strengths. Because of Jesus, I found purpose for my life—to tell others about Him. I want everyone to know His love, forgiveness, and gift of eternal life.

Nicodemus: Would you say that He is the Son of God?

Peter: Yes, I would.

Caiaphas: Your honor, this witness is of questionable character. I have witnesses who claim that he denied Jesus three times the night before Jesus was killed. How do we know he is telling the truth now?

Peter: It is true. I denied Jesus on the night He needed my support. However, Jesus forgave me and reassured me that He still loves me. This forgiveness is available not only for me, but for anyone who asks.

Nicodemus: Thank you, Peter. I would like to call as a witness, the disciple Matthew. Matthew, please tell the court about your relationship with Jesus.

Matthew: *(walks up with Bible in hand)* I was a tax collector until I met Jesus. Jesus accepted me when others rejected me. Using my recording talents, I kept notes of all Jesus said and did. I submit them to this court in the form of a book, the Gospel according to Matthew. *(presents Bible to judge)* This book gives testimony to the fact that Jesus is the Son of God.

Nicodemus: Thank you, Matthew. Next, we have a woman who was a follower of Jesus and traveled quite extensively with Him. The defense calls Mary Magdalene to the stand. *(Matthew exits, and Mary enters the witness stand.)*

Caiaphas: I object to this witness. First of all, she is a woman, which makes her testimony questionable. But most of all, she has a history of being possessed by demons. How do we know it is she speaking and not one of the demons inside her?

Nicodemus: Your honor, it is true that she had seven demons. But she was healed by Jesus. And as far as her being a woman, Jesus showed us that we can all serve Him.

Judge: *(slams gavel)* Proceed with the questioning of this witness.

Nicodemus: Mary, please tell the court about Christ's resurrection and how it proves He is the Son of God.

Mary: Nicodemus was correct in his description of me before I met Jesus. I had seven demons, but Jesus healed me. I was so grateful that I followed and traveled with Him and the disciples. Jesus accepted me, and I became totally devoted to Him. John and I were among the few followers present at the cross. I was also the first to see Him after He arose from the dead. I will never forget that morning. He called me by name and told me to go and tell the other disciples that He was alive. I know Jesus is the Son of God, that He arose from the dead, and that He loves me just as I am. I also know He loves each one of us.

Nicodemus: Thank you, Mary. After Jesus arose and ascended into Heaven, He challenged the remaining disciples to go tell people about Him. Many religious leaders refuse to accept Jesus as the Christ; they have been persecuting Jesus' followers. I would like to place into evidence a letter submitted by Philip, the Evangelist. Philip is one of the seven who were appointed to help the apostles spread the good news of Christ. Philip provides testimony from his friend, Stephen. *(Nicodemus gives the letter to judge.)*

Judge: *(opens letter and reads)* Honorable Judge, I would like to share the story of my close friend who was killed for his belief. Stephen helped to distribute food and care for the widows in our Christian community. He also preached and taught. Members of the synagogue were angered by his teachings about Jesus. They brought him to trial. Stephen gave his testimony, explaining how God worked through our Jewish history preparing His people for the Messiah. He said the synagogue leaders had wrongly crucified Jesus. The leaders were so furious they stoned him. Stephen prayed for forgiveness for those who were stoning him to death. Your honor, we believe Jesus to be the Son to God. We will suffer so that others can know and believe in Jesus. Respectfully, Philip the Evangelist.

Nicodemus: The next witness I call to the stand is the Apostle Paul. *(Paul takes the stand.)*

Caiaphas: Your honor, how can you allow this witness? Paul isn't even his real name. I know him as Saul. I also know him to be a murderer. He was present and approved the stoning of Stephen whose testimony you just read.

Judge: Nicodemus, is this true?

Paul: Please your honor, let me answer those accusations. Yes, my name was Saul of Tarsus. I was a leader in the synagogue and planned the deaths of many Christians. But Jesus appeared to me while I was on my way to Damascus to capture some followers of Christ. I was stopped by a blinding light. A voice asked, "Why do you persecute me?" I realized it was Jesus Christ speaking to me. Later, a man named Ananias met me and helped me obey Jesus. I continued to learn from faithful men like Barnabas about the love, mercy and forgiveness of Jesus. I am proof that Christ can change a life. I am called to be a missionary, sharing the love of Christ to all. The message of God's love and forgiveness is for everyone. Because I preach about Jesus, I have been in prison. In fact, I am here in chains today. *(Lift up hands to show chains.)*

Nicodemus: Thank you for that testimony, Paul. I have one more witness. Priscilla, could you please tell the court why you and your husband consider yourselves witnesses for Christ?

Caiaphas: Your honor, I object to this witness because she never met Jesus when He was alive. How can she give witness to someone she did not meet?

Nicodemus: Your honor, we did not know Abraham, yet we believe in him and all that he taught us about God. We did not know Moses, yet we live by the laws that he received from God. I argue that one doesn't have to experience something first-hand to give witness to it. I am asking Priscilla to answer how knowing about Jesus has affected her life personally. She can give testimony to this.

Judge: *(slam gavel)* Objection overruled. Proceed with the witness.

Priscilla: My husband, Aquilla, and I came to know Christ through Paul. He told us the good news of Christ. We use our house as a place people can learn about Jesus. Many times our faith has put our lives at risk, but we know this message of Jesus Christ is true. It is worth any persecution we may endure.

Nicodemus: Your honor, I would like to close the case for the defense with a few thoughts. I am a religious leader. I knew Jesus and, at first, I too questioned His authority. I came to Him at night so that other religious leaders would not see me. I wanted to know how to enter the kingdom of God. Jesus explained to me how God loved us so much that He sent His Son, Jesus, into the world to save the world. He promises that whoever believes in Him would have eternal life. I believe Jesus to be the true Son of God. *(Nicodemus sits down.)*

Judge: We will take a recess until Monday, and then I will make a ruling on this case based on the evidence presented. Court adjourned. *(slam gavel)*

Witnesses of Today

Circle the people who can be witnesses of their faith in Christ.
Write one way they could share their faith.

Minister

_____

_____

_____

Soccer Coach

_____

_____

_____

Teacher

_____

_____

_____

Missionary

_____

_____

_____

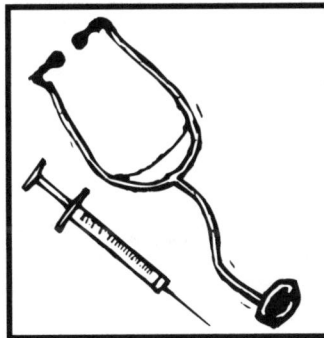

Nurse

_____

_____

_____

Sunday School Teacher

_____

_____

_____

Who has been a witness for Christ to you?

Family Feedback

Parent interviews preteen using questions below.
After preteen responds, parent also answers the question.

1. What is your favorite holiday?

2. What is your favorite color?

3. What is your favorite school subject?

4. Who has been your favorite teacher?

5. Name two of your best friends.

6. Name a favorite TV show?

7. What is the best present you have ever received?

8. Tell about a time you were really happy.

9. Tell about a time you were angry.

10. What makes you feel sad?

11. What is your favorite fact about God?

12. If you could ask God any question, what would you ask Him?

Dear parent: This week we talked about New Testament heroes who shared their faith in Christ. The purpose of this sheet is to help your preteen share things that are important to him or her. Learning to share important things will help your preteen to share his or her faith in Christ.

Getting to Know You

Aim. To provide opportunities for parent and child interaction and for parents to hear the message of Jesus Christ.

Get Into the Game

Use one or both of these activities to begin this session.

Activity #1—Bible Costume Game

Divide students and parents into teams of approximately six to eight members. Each team "dresses up" one team member, creating a Bible character using props of paper table coverings and toilet paper.

Materials

rolls of toilet paper, roll of paper table coverings, tape, string

Activity #2—FAITH Game

Copy "Faith" game cards and calling cards. This game is played like BINGO. Have students form groups of two or three players with their parents and give each group a game card. The teacher draws and reads one calling card Bible hero name at a time. The groups cover the hero name called with a marker or bean. The first card to have five in a row scores a FAITH. As a review, ask students to give information about the hero that is called. (Option: This game could be used for future review. Laminate cards or cover with contact paper to make them more durable.)

Materials

photocopies of pages 117–122, markers or dried beans, calling cards cut apart and put into a container

Step 1

Select students in advance to present the play from Session 4. Assign parts for them to practice (pages 109–112). They should be familiar with the script but they need not memorize their parts. Arrange the room as directed in the script. Since this play uses only ten students, you may want to write in other parts or add a jury so that all students can participate. If you have fewer than ten students, one student could take more than one part or a character could be omitted. Provide props (i.e., robe for judge, Bible costumes for characters).

Materials
photocopies of pages 109–112

Step 2

Select in advance two or three parents to each give a three-minute testimony about their faith in Christ. Introduce this section by explaining that we not only have testimonies from New Testament characters, but we also have testimonies from today of how Jesus can change our lives.

Take It to the Next Level

The minister or other selected leader will offer a devotion appropriate for both parents and preteens explaining how to accept Christ as Savior and Lord. (Suggestion: This might be an appropriate time to talk with parents or children who want to make a commitment. Also have Bibles or other information available to give them.) Close with refreshments and a time for fellowship.

(Note: Include students whose parents are not able to come. If you have more than one in this situation, have them work together or team them up with other families.)

Calling Cards

Cut apart the calling cards. Mix them up in a coffee can or paper bag.
Randomly pick a card and call the letter and the hero name. Student covers heroes that are on his card.

(F) ADAM	(A) EVE	(I) ABEL	(T) NOAH	(H) ABRAHAM
(F) SARAH	(A) ISAAC	(I) JACOB	(T) JOSEPH	(H) MIRIAM
(F) MOSES	(A) RAHAB	(I) JOSHUA	(T) DEBORAH	(H) GIDEON
(F) SAMSON	(A) RUTH	(I) HANNAH	(T) SAMUEL	(H) ELI
(F) SAUL	(A) DAVID	(I) SOLOMON	(T) ELIJAH	(H) AHAB
(F) JEZEBEL	(A) JONAH	(I) ISAIAH	(T) DAVID	(H) KING NEBUCHAD-NEZZAR
(F) KING DARIUS	(A) ESTHER	(I) MORDECAI	(T) KING XERXES	(H) NEHEMIAH
(F) JOHN THE BAPTIST	(A) NICODEMUS	(I) JESUS	(T) PETER	(H) MATTHEW
(F) MARY MAGDALENE	(A) STEPHEN	(I) PAUL	(T) PRISCILLA	(H) AQUILA
(F) ABIGAIL	(A) JOSIAH	(I) ASA	(T) CAIN	(H) DELILAH

Card 1

F	A	I	T	H
Adam	Isaac	Joshua	Samuel	Abraham
Moses	Rahab	Hannah	Elijah	Gideon
Saul	David	FREE SPACE	King Xerxes	Nehemiah
Jezebel	Jonah	Isaiah	Peter	Matthew
John the Baptist	Nicodemus	Paul	Cain	Aquila

Card 2

F	A	I	T	H
Mary Magdalene	Jonah	Isaiah	Cain	Eli
Sarah	Eve	Abel	Noah	Gideon
Abigail	Esther	FREE SPACE	Deborah	Ahab
Saul	Nicodemus	Paul	Joseph	Miriam
Samson	Stephen	Mordecai	David	Matthew

Card 3

F	A	I	T	H
Jezebel	Moses	King Darius	Abigail	Samson
Stephen	Rahab	Esther	Josiah	Nicodemus
Isaiah	Jacob	FREE SPACE	Asa	Mordecai
Daniel	Noah	Samuel	Cain	Deborah
Matthew	Eli	Ahab	Delilah	Nehemiah

Card 4

F	A	I	T	H
Mary Magdalene	Eve	Abel	Elijah	Abraham
Sarah	Ruth	Solomon	Peter	Miriam
John the Baptist	Jonah	FREE SPACE	King Xerxes	Gideon
Saul	David	Hannah	Joseph	Aquila
Adam	Isaac	Joshua	Samuel	Ahab

Card 1

F	A	I	T	H
Samson	Ruth	Hannah	Samuel	Eli
Abigail	Josiah	Asa	Cain	Delilah
King Darius	Jonah	FREE SPACE	Priscilla	Matthew
Moses	Rahab	Joshua	Deborah	Gideon
Jezebel	David	Isaiah	Daniel	King Nebuchadnezzar

Card 2

F	A	I	T	H
John the Baptist	Nicodemus	Jesus	Peter	Matthew
Saul	David	Solomon	Elijah	Ahab
Abigail	Josiah	FREE SPACE	Cain	Aquila
Sarah	Isaac	Jacob	Joseph	Miriam
Moses	Rahab	Mordecai	King Xerxes	Nehemiah

Card 3

F	A	I	T	H
Moses	Rahab	Joshua	Deborah	Gideon
Abigail	Josiah	Asa	Cain	Delilah
King Darius	Esther	FREE SPACE	Peter	Matthew
Jezebel	Jonah	Isaiah	David	King Nebuchadnezzar
Saul	David	Mordecai	Priscilla	Eli

Card 4

F	A	I	T	H
Jezebel	Stephen	Asa	Elijah	Abraham
John the Baptist	Ruth	Hannah	Peter	Nehemiah
Adam	Isaac	FREE SPACE	Isaiah	Eli
Mary Magdalene	Esther	Jesus	Noah	Aquila
Sarah	Nicodemus	Paul	Joseph	Miriam

FAITH Bingo Cards

F	A	I	T	H
Adam	Isaac	Abel	Joseph	Gideon
Samson	David	Hannah	Elijah	Nehemiah
Mary Magdalene	Esther	FREE SPACE	Noah	Eli
Saul	Jonah	Solomon	Daniel	Matthew
Jezebel	Ruth	Jacob	Peter	Aquila

F	A	I	T	H
Sarah	Rahab	Joshua	Samuel	Abraham
Moses	Nicodemus	Paul	King Xerxes	Delilah
Abigail	Josiah	FREE SPACE	Priscilla	Ahab
King Darius	Eve	Asa	Cain	Aquila
John the Baptist	Stephen	Mordecai	Noah	Miriam

F	A	I	T	H
Adam	Isaac	Joshua	Samuel	Ahab
Moses	Eve	Mordecai	Daniel	Eli
Samson	Ruth	FREE SPACE	Elijah	Gideon
Abigail	Stephen	Jesus	King Xerxes	King Nebuchadnezzar
John the Baptist	Esther	Isaiah	Deborah	Abraham

F	A	I	T	H
Jezebel	Jonah	Solomon	Elijah	Ahab
Samson	Ruth	Hannah	Deborah	Gideon
Saul	Josiah	FREE SPACE	Cain	Matthew
King Darius	Esther	Asa	Peter	Eli
Sarah	David	Jacob	Noah	Aquila

Card 1

F	A	I	T	H
Adam	Josiah	Abel	Cain	Abraham
Abigail	Eve	Asa	Noah	Delilah
Sarah	Stephen	FREE SPACE	Joseph	Aquila
Mary Magdalene	Isaac	Paul	Deborah	Matthew
Saul	Esther	Hannah	Daniel	Eli

Card 2

F	A	I	T	H
Samson	Nicodemus	Isaiah	Elijah	Ahab
Moses	Ruth	Jacob	Samuel	Nehemiah
John the Baptist	Jonah	FREE SPACE	Peter	Gideon
Abigail	David	Asa	King Xerxes	Eli
King Darius	Rahab	Joshua	Priscilla	Abraham

Card 3

F	A	I	T	H
King Darius	Esther	Mordecai	King Xerxes	Nehemiah
John the Baptist	Nicodemus	Jesus	Peter	Matthew
Mary Magdalene	Stephen	FREE SPACE	Priscilla	Aquila
Sarah	Isaac	Jacob	Joseph	Miriam
Saul	David	Solomon	Elijah	Ahab

Card 4

F	A	I	T	H
Samson	Ruth	Joshua	Deborah	Gideon
Moses	Rahab	Hannah	Samuel	Eli
Adam	Eve	FREE SPACE	Noah	Abraham
Abigail	Jonah	Abel	Daniel	Ahab
Jezebel	Josiah	Isaiah	Cain	Matthew

F	A	I	T	H
		FREE SPACE		

F	A	I	T	H
		FREE SPACE		

F	A	I	T	H
		FREE SPACE		

F	A	I	T	H
		FREE SPACE		

Share Your Faith

Get Into the Game

As students arrive, give them each a sheet of paper, glue, and yarn. Students think of a word that describes themselves and spell it with yarn glued to the paper. See example in margin.

After they are finished, give them time to tell why they chose their word. Say, "Today we will learn to share something else—our faith in Christ."

Materials
construction paper, glue, yarn

Step 1

Before class, prepare the following gift bags as follows. Make signs as directed on large sheets of paper.

Say, "In Session 4, we learned about New Testament heroes who shared their faith. We called them witnesses because they gave 'witness' to something they believed was true." Have students find Matthew 28:19, 20 and read aloud. Then ask the following questions:

1. What does Jesus tell us to do? (He commands us to make disciples and then teach them.)

Materials
gift bags, two red paper hearts, Lego blocks, a small gift-wrapped package, praying hands (statue, picture, or made from paper), picture of Jesus (sticker or picture), large sheets of paper, masking tape

2. What will we teach? (The message of God's love and Jesus' death, burial, and resurrection that provides the promise of eternal life.)

3. What does it mean to share our faith and be a witness for Christ?

Explain to the students, "We can be a witness and share our faith in many ways. First of all, we can share our faith by living the way God wants us to and doing the right things. People will recognize that there is something different about us. We can also share our faith by looking to the interests of others and helping people. People will see our unselfishness. Finally, we can be witnesses by telling our friends about Jesus or by inviting our friends to church so they can hear about Jesus. No matter how we choose to be a witness, there will come a time when someone will ask us what we believe. How should we answer someone who asks, 'What is a Christian?' Let's look up verses to help us with this." Use six volunteers to open gifts and post signs as directed. The remaining students will read the verses aloud.

Bag #1

Read 1 John 4:9. Say, "God loved us so much, He sent His one and only Son, Jesus, to earth so that we might have a right relationship with God and receive eternal life . . . living with God forever."

(Student opens first bag, holds up heart and tapes the first sign to the wall under the ceiling. Class repeats, "God loves me.")

Bag #2

Read Romans 3:23. Say, "What is sin? Sin is doing things our own way and not caring what God thinks. It is disobeying His laws that help us live correctly and safely. All of us have sinned. We have been selfish and cared about ourselves more than pleasing God. It does not matter if it is a sin such as lying, or a sin such as murdering; all disobedience is sin. God is holy, and He cannot live with sin. Sin separates us from God. There is nothing we can do to take away our own sin. God says sin must be punished. We cannot have eternal life with Him if there is a wall of sin between us."

(Student opens bag #2, holds up Lego block wall, and tapes second sign under previous sign. Class repeats, "I am a sinner.")

Bag #3

Read Romans 5:8. Say, "Even though we are sinners, God loves us. God sent His Son, Jesus, to earth to restore our friendship with Him. Jesus never sinned. He is the perfect sacrifice, taking our sins on himself so that our sins are blotted out.

Bag #1
Large red paper heart

> God loves me.
> 1 John 4:9

Bag #2
Lego blocks put together to make a small wall

> I am a sinner.
> Romans 3:23

Bag #3
Fifteen Lego blocks, not put together

> Jesus died for my sins.
> Romans 5:8

Bag #4
Praying hands (statue, picture, or cut from paper)

> I can be forgiven.
> 1 John 1:9

Bag #5
Large red construction paper heart with a picture of Jesus in the center

> I can live forever
> with Jesus.
> Romans 6:23

Bag #6
Gift-wrapped package

> God will help me
> every day.
> Romans 8:28

When Jesus died on the cross, He broke down the wall that sin had built up between us and God. Because of Jesus, we have forgiveness for our sins and a right relationship with God."

(Student opens bag #3, dumps out Lego blocks on the floor to symbolize the wall has been broken down. Tape sign under previous sign. Class repeats, "Jesus died for my sins.")

Bag #4

Read 1 John 1:9. Say, "When Jesus died on the cross, His offer of forgiveness tore down the wall of sin between us and God. However, we have to ask to receive this forgiveness. When we ask Jesus to forgive us our sin, He will! He will forgive us, tear down the wall of sin, and make us right with God. We will still do wrong things sometimes, but that wall is torn down so that we can always have a relationship with God."

(Student opens bag #4, holds up praying hands and tapes sign under previous sign. Class repeats, "I can be forgiven.")

Bag #5

Read Romans 6:23. Say, "Not only does God give us forgiveness for our sins, He also gives us eternal life in a personal relationship with His Son, Jesus. His Spirit lives with us and gives us help and support. When we are lonely, we can always know that He is with us. He will never leave us. He is our best friend for life!"

(Student opens bag #5 and holds up heart with picture of Jesus. Student tapes sign under previous sign. Class repeats: "I can live forever with Jesus.")

Bag #6

Read Romans 8:28. Say, "Another gift we receive is help to live everyday. We know we can live with God our King forever in Heaven, but we know that God also helps us every day."

(Student opens bag #6 and holds up a gift-wrapped package, tapes new sign under previous sign. Class repeats, "God will help me every day.")

When I became a Christian, I learned that . . .

(Point to signs on wall. Have class repeat.)

Step 2

Explain to the students, "We are going to make a bookmark to help us remember what we've just learned. You can keep this in your Bible for review. This bookmark could be used to help you share your faith with others."

Make a sample using the bookmark pattern on page 127. Give each student a piece of tag board or poster board and

Materials
tag board or poster board, small stickers of Jesus, colored markers, hole punch, yarn or embroidery thread, page 127

markers or colored pencils. Students decorate the bookmarks. Use yarn or embroidery thread to make a tassel. To make even more durable, cover with clear adhesive plastic.

Step 3

Divide into groups of four or five students and one adult leader. Read and discuss the following situations.

Materials
cut apart photocopies of page 128

1. Annalisa is new in the neighborhood. Allyson noticed that she didn't go to church, so she invited her to Vacation Bible School. The last night of VBS, the minister shared how Christ changed his life and invited anyone to come forward who would like to become a Christian. Annalisa asked Allyson what this meant. How can Allyson explain this to Annalisa?

(Christ wants to have a relationship with us, and His Spirit can live in our hearts and be with us always. We can accept Him into our lives.)

2. Jared is afraid of dying. He doesn't know what happens after people die, and he is afraid. He told this to his friend Jordan. What can Jordan tell Jared about eternal life that would help him?

(Jordan can tell Jared about the promise of eternal life and how to receive it. Jordan can assure Jared that this message of Heaven is true because Jesus promised it to be available to all who believe and obey in Him.)

3. Jonathan was playing with matches and accidentally caught part of his house on fire. No one was hurt, and the insurance money helped fix the damage. However, there were some items lost that could not be replaced. This hurt his mother deeply. Jonathan felt very sorry about this. It has been a year, and he still feels very guilty. He confided in his best friend, Caroline. What can she tell Jonathan about Christ that can help him with his guilt?

(Caroline can share how Christ has forgiven Jonathan, and he can let go of his past and not feel guilty. Jesus doesn't want us to carry guilt: sin is the reason He died on the cross. We have the promise that we are indeed forgiven.)

Take It to the Next Level

Challenge students to take their bookmarks home and explain them to their parents. This will help students review the basics of their faith. Close the session with prayer.

Bookmark

Cut out both copies of this bookmark and trace the bookmark shape onto heavy paper. Cut out. Glue the bookmarks to the heavy paper.

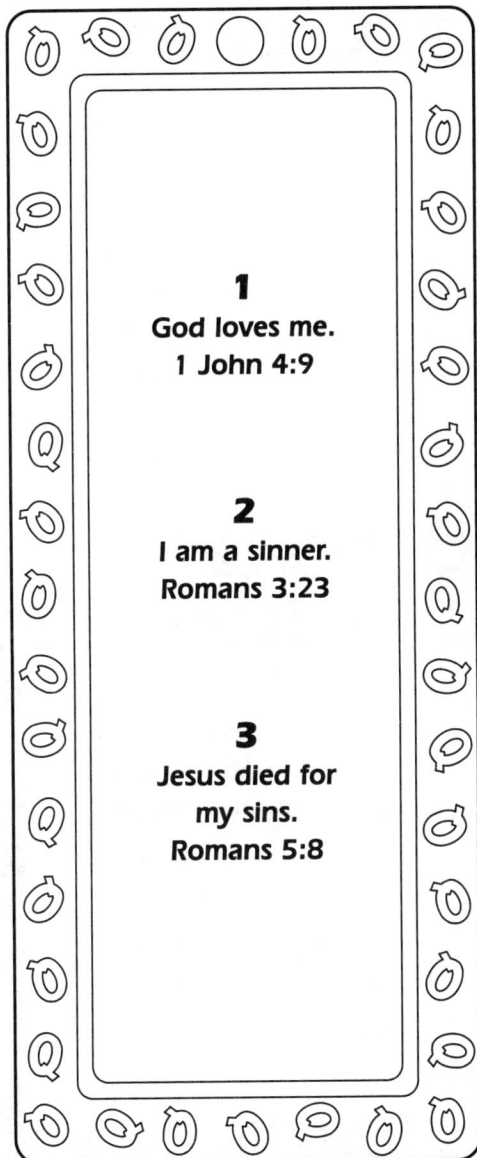

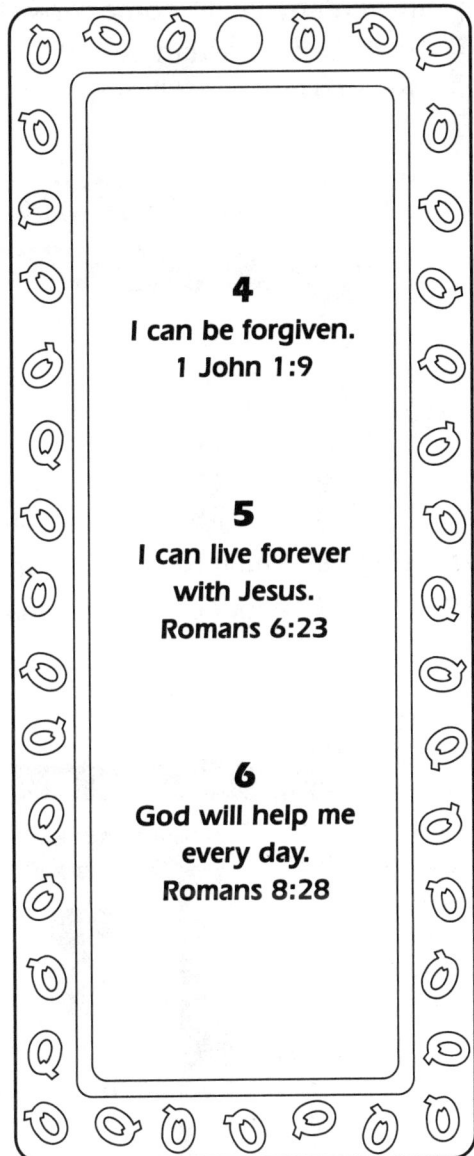

1

God loves me.
1 John 4:9

2

I am a sinner.
Romans 3:23

3

Jesus died for
my sins.
Romans 5:8

4

I can be forgiven.
1 John 1:9

5

I can live forever
with Jesus.
Romans 6:23

6

God will help me
every day.
Romans 8:28

1 Annalisa is new in the neighborhood. Allyson noticed that she didn't go to church, so she invited her to Vacation Bible School. The last night of VBS, the minister shared how Christ changed his life and invited anyone to come forward who would like to become a Christian. Annalisa asked Allyson what this meant. How can Allyson explain this to Annalisa?

2 Jared is afraid of dying. He doesn't know what happens after people die, and he is afraid. He told this to his friend Jordan. What can Jordan tell Jared about eternal life that would help him?

3 Jonathan was playing with matches and accidentally caught part of his house on fire. No one was hurt, and the insurance money helped fix the damage. However, there were some items lost that could not be replaced. This hurt his mother deeply. Jonathan felt very sorry about this. It has been a year, and he still feels very guilty. He confided in his best friend, Caroline. What can she tell Jonathan about Christ that can help him with his guilt?